MW01047185

Romanticism's Child

Romanticism's Child

*An Intellectual History of James Tod's
Influence on Indian History and
Historiography*

Lloyd I. Rudolph
Susanne Hoeber Rudolph

OXFORD
UNIVERSITY PRESS

OXFORD
UNIVERSITY PRESS

Oxford University Press is a department of the University of Oxford.
It furthers the University's objective of excellence in research, scholarship,
and education by publishing worldwide. Oxford is a registered trademark of
Oxford University Press in the UK and in certain other countries.

Published in India by
Oxford University Press
YMCA Library Building, 1 Jai Singh Road, New Delhi 110 001, India

First Edition published in 2017

ISBN-13: 978-0-19-946589-7
ISBN-10: 0-19-946589-4

Typeset in Goudy Old Style 11/16
by Tranistics Data Technologies, Kolkata 700091
Printed in India by Replika Press Pvt. Ltd

Contents

Foreword

Across the broad New England lawn punctuated by high maple trees, the lovely white clapboard house stood comfortably in the mid-July sunshine. My wife and I had driven up from Philadelphia to the village of Barnard, Vermont, as we had every year for so many summers. We were once again visiting my sister, Susanne, and Lloyd, her husband of 63 years. They had both been in declining health for a long time and it seemed likely that this would be our last visit to the residence to which they retired to write and relax in the warm months each year since 1960. We passed under the dark green leaves of the Dutchman's pipe vine shading the front door and entered the large living room. The big fireplace of river boulders that hosted a roaring fire in winter was now cool and quiet. The far side of the living room opened onto the sunlit porch that stretched along the far side of the house. The porch was the center of summer life in the house, with generous windows looking onto the green hillside that sloped down to the gentle waters of Silver Lake. Susanne and Lloyd sat close together at the wooden table facing the lawn and the lake. The table was littered with typescripts, pens and pencils, books, newspapers, slips of paper with handwritten notes, and two laptop computers side by side—a mix of things that reflected intense work and the Rudolphs' complex creative process. They interrupted their conversation and with bright smiles welcomed us once again into their home and workplace, just as they had welcomed countless other friends, relatives, colleagues, and students over the course of their lives together. The papers on the table in that lovely spot were the working materials for the book you are holding. No matter how unwell they became, Susanne and Lloyd were enlivened and invigorated by their joint work—work through which they brought to the world the lectures, articles, and books they wrote together in their unique lifetime partnership. We were sad to see them in poor health, but were moved by the fact that their work continued to drive them cheerfully forward to the very end.

Susanne and Lloyd's health continued to decline in the weeks after we visited them in Vermont, and six months later they were gone. Susanne died on December 23, 2015, and Lloyd just 23 days later, on January 16, 2016. One of their last wishes was to see this book in print.

* * *

Lloyd Irving Rudolph was born in Chicago, Illinois, on November 1, 1927. After graduating from high school, he was appointed a cadet at West Point in 1945, but resigned his appointment after a semester to attend Harvard University, from where he graduated magna cum laude in 1948. From Harvard he also earned a master of public administration degree in 1950 and a PhD in political science in 1956.

Susanne Hoeber Rudolph was born in Mannheim, Germany, on April 3, 1930. She was the daughter of educated Social Democratic activists who fled Hitler's Germany just before World War II; Susanne was nine when she came to the United States. She graduated from Sarah Lawrence College and earned her Harvard PhD in 1955.

Susanne and Lloyd's marriage in 1952 launched an exceptional personal and professional partnership that endured for more than six decades. Because they wrote and published together and often taught and lectured together, they were mostly referred to in a single collective noun: "The Rudolphs." Aside from their academic work, the Rudolphs were revered for their hospitality, which epitomized their thoughtful, caring approach to their students, colleagues, research subjects, and friends. They regularly hosted interesting guests over generous meals that ranged from a quiet, elegant French dinner for four at their large, old Chicago house to parties for more than a hundred featuring fine Indian food or a traditional New England country supper on the lawn of their Vermont summer home. Even more, the Rudolphs were open to conversations with students and colleagues about everything they were doing. They showed endless interest in the research, writing, and analysis that others were carrying out. At any visit to their home, one was likely to encounter not just academics but also journalists, politicians, and other public figures from India and other countries as well as Americans. A remarkable characteristic of the many tributes published after the Rudolphs died was the number of individuals who felt they had a "special" relationship with the Rudolphs that no one else shared. Prominent individuals in academia and politics from around the world remarked on how the Rudolphs had opened new worlds of study and ideas to them. They were admired for how they lived as well as for how they thought, wrote, and taught. They were seen not only as brilliant and scintillating but also as engaged, warm, and compassionate. Between them, they supervised some 300 doctoral dissertations.

The Rudolphs joined the Harvard faculty upon their return from their first trip to India in 1957. They remained there until 1964, when they were appointed to the University of Chicago political science faculty. It was even more unusual then than it would be today for both a husband and wife to be appointed to tenure track positions at the same university, in the same department, and at the same time. At the University of Chicago, Lloyd served as Chair of the Committee on

International Relations and the Master of Arts Program in the Social Sciences and as Chair of concentrations in political science, public policy, international studies, and South Asian studies in the College. In 1999, Lloyd Rudolph received the University's Faculty Award for Excellence in Graduate Teaching.

Susanne became the William Benton Distinguished Service Professor of Political Science at the University. She was elected president of the 13,000-member American Political Science Association and the Association for Asian Studies, and was a member of the American Academy of Arts and Sciences. In recognition of her dedication to her students, she was awarded the Llewellyn John and Harriet Manchester Quantrell Award for Excellence in Undergraduate Teaching.

The Rudolphs were active in the "Perestroika" movement within the political science field, a loose-knit grassroots effort in the early 2000s that sought to open political science to greater methodological pluralism. The Rudolphs received the 2009 Blade of Grass Award, given by the Interpretive Methodologies and Methods Conference Group of the American Political Science Association, in honor of their contributions to interpretive studies of the political world.

The Rudolphs first travelled to India in 1956 in an adventurous journey, driving overland from Germany to Delhi in a Land Rover. That adventure was recounted in one of their last books, *Destination India* (2014).[1] On this first visit to India, they spent several months in Jaipur and the surrounding area, developing an interest in and love for Rajasthan that would bring them back frequently. After this 1956–57 sojourn, they returned to India every third or fourth year, bringing their three children with them and so they all grew up learning Hindi. After their retirement from active teaching in 2002, the Rudolphs returned to Jaipur each winter for several months of continued research and writing and to renew connections with Indian officials, scholars, and friends. In 2014, on their last trip to India, the Rudolphs were both presented the Padma Bhushan award, one of India's highest civilian honors, by President Pranab Mukherjee. The award recognizes distinguished service of a high order to the nation of India.

The Rudolphs between them published more than 20 books and dozens of articles. They co-authored or co-edited eight books together, starting with *The Modernity of Tradition* (1967),[2] a seminal formulation of the problem of tradition and modernity that shaped the study of India's past and present over the next 50 years. It turned out to be one of the most enduring interpretations of modernization not just of Indian society but also of non-Western nations around the world. At a time when reigning theories of the 1950s blamed the "backwardness" of India on the tenacity of her "traditional" institutions like caste, the Rudolphs showed how traditional-seeming institutions had actually changed through the colonial period to take on functions similar to political parties that one could only see as "modern."

Their later work on Indian capitalism, Gandhi, and other topics were similarly informed by a deep sensitivity to India's specific history and culture. Their other books include *Education and Politics in India* (1972); *The Regional Imperative: The Administration of U.S. Foreign Policy Towards South Asian States* (1980, 2007), *Gandhi: The Traditional Roots of Charisma* (1983); *In Pursuit of Lakshmi: The Political Economy of the Indian State* (1987); and *Postmodern Gandhi and Other Essays* (2006). In 2008, Oxford University Press published a three-volume, career-spanning collection of the Rudolphs' writings titled *Explaining Indian Democracy: A Fifty-Year Perspective, 1956–2006*.[3]

From the beginning, the Rudolphs had a particular interest in Rajasthan's history and politics and were keen observers of its changing role in the Indian constellation from its singular position under British imperial rule to the controversies of the present day. Their *Essays on Rajputana* (1984),[4] incorporating essays written over 20 years, treated issues of history, politics, ethnography, and sociology in this part of India. The preface to that volume included this important note:

> Our research in Rajputana was significantly affected when, in 1970, the late Colonel Kesri Singh called our attention to the forty-four year diary of his eldest brother, Thakur Amar Singh of Kanota. Between 1898 when he was eighteen until his death in 1942, Amar Singh daily wrote extensive accounts of his life and times. The diary, bound in eighty-seven folio size volumes of about eight hundred pages each, resides these days in Kanota fort. Since beginning our work on the diary, the spirit of Amar Singh has lived with us.

Amar Singh and his 70,000-page diary would indeed live with them for many more years, until they were finally able to publish their analysis of the diarist's observations, *Reversing the Gaze: Amar Singh's Diary–A Colonial Subject's Narrative of Imperial India* (2000).[5]

The topic of James Tod has been of interest to the Rudolphs since their earliest engagement with Rajasthan. Shortly after their return from India in 1957, they were on a visit to Susanne's family in Philadelphia when they discovered a first edition of *The Annals and Antiquities of Rajasthan* on the dusty shelves of an antiquarian bookshop near Rittenhouse Square. They were unable to afford it themselves, but Susanne's parents made them a gift of it, the two volumes rebound in bright reddish buckram to replace the crumbled original leather binding. When the Rudolphs died nearly 60 years later, the two volumes—the bindings now faded and worn to dull beige—still occupied a prominent place in their apartment. The printed pages remain bright and clear and the magnificent illustrations look as though they were printed yesterday.

The Rudolphs' intentions with respect to the book you are holding are expressed in notes they left among their research materials. One instructive (undated) note reads as follows:

Few persons have had the kind of impact on the Indian popular nationalist imagination that James Tod (1782–1835) has had. Tod's words and images have echoed in prose and verse, been amplified in pamphlet and history and have resounded in theatre and podium. His has been a powerful, but essentially underestimated, influence. In an extraordinary afterlife Tod's writing has animated popular Indian nationalism through the nineteenth and twentieth centuries. He was among the first scholars who shifted Orientalist interest from the classical to the vernacular, from the written to the oral tradition, from the Brahman to the bard. He made the three figures of Prithviraj, Padmini, and Pratap iconic to the vernacular nationalist imaginary. Tod's work was inspirational to the literary modernity of several Indian languages including Bengali, Rajasthani, and Hindi. Ironically, although Tod's persona exemplified colonialism, it shaped powerfully the aesthetic of anti-colonial praxis and continues to inspire militant nationalist ideologies.

The Rudolphs regarded Tod as a seminal figure for the history and historiography of British colonialism in India; for the development of the "martial race" ideology of the Victorian empire in India after 1857; for the narratives, images, and vernacular literature of the Indian nationalist movement; for the construction of Rajput identity; and for the history and historiography of Rajasthan. Despite such important potential contributions to knowledge about India, they noted that James Tod finds no place in standard reference works such as Volume I, "The Founders," of Philip Woodruff's *The Men Who Ruled India* (1953); Parshotam Mehra's *A Dictionary of Modern Indian History, 1707–1947* (1985); or Surjit Mansingh's *Historical Dictionary of India* (1996).[6] The Rudolphs hoped to help fill this scholarly lacuna by bringing out this volume of essays and documents on James Tod.

The Rudolphs also sought to contribute to post-colonial analysis and interpretation. They observed that Tod scholarship has tended to be confined to the regional history of Rajasthan, although more recently it has begun to find a place in colonial history and in post-colonial studies. For example, Ramya Sreenivasan's *The Many Lives of a Rajput Queen: Heroic Pasts in India, 1500–1900* (2007) and Cynthia Talbot's *The Last Hindu Emperor: Prithviraj Chauhan and the Indian Past, 1200–2000* (2016) relate Tod's text and its influence to nationalist discourses and Hindu and Muslim narratives and imagery.[7] It is being increasingly recognized that Tod's text has played a key role in what might be called a vernacular orientalism—an orientalism that differs from the civilizational orientalism of Sir William Jones and his colleagues at the Asiatic Society of Bengal and the Saidian orientalism of post-colonial scholars. Interpretations of the heroes whose tales Tod narrated, for example, Prithviraj, Padmini, and Rana Pratap, can be found in modern Hindi, Bengali, and Rajasthani plays, poetry, and literature, and even in contemporary Amar Chitra Katha comic books. This book is intended to show Tod's significance for colonial and post-colonial scholarship and for the broader terrain of historical and contemporary popular consciousness.

* * *

A final point: the Rudolphs' five essays that make up Part I of this book contain some duplication and overlap. Thus, the same point might be made in two or three of the chapters, sometimes even with similar wording. In the final analysis, this may be regarded as a strength of this book as much as a weakness. The Rudolphs wrote and rewrote these essays over a period of more than 40 years and considered and reconsidered certain points from various perspectives over time. Perhaps, had they lived longer, they might have in some way reconciled the duplications that appear in these essays before publication. As it is, however, the reader will gain insight into the development of their thinking over time by having the chance to read their consideration of similar issues in differing contexts.

Francis W. Hoeber
Philadelphia, 2016

Notes

1.   Lloyd I. Rudolph and Susanne Hoeber Rudolph, *Destination India: From London Overland to India and What We Learned There* (New Delhi: Oxford University Press, 2014).

2.   Lloyd I. Rudolph and Susanne Hoeber Rudolph, *The Modernity of Tradition: Political Development in India* (Chicago: University of Chicago Press, 1967).

3.   Lloyd I. Rudolph and Susanne Hoeber Rudolph (with Paul R. Brass), *Education and Politics in India: Studies in Organization, Society, and Policy* (Cambridge: Harvard University Press, 1972); Lloyd I. Rudolph and Susanne Hoeber Rudolph, *The Regional Imperative: The Administration of U.S. Foreign Policy Towards South Asian States* (New

Delhi: Concept Publishing Company, 1980, 2007); Lloyd I. Rudolph and Susanne Hoeber Rudolph, *Gandhi: The Traditional Roots of Charisma* (Chicago: University of Chicago Press, 1983); Lloyd I. Rudolph and Susanne Hoeber Rudolph, *In Pursuit of Lakshmi: The Political Economy of the Indian State* (Chicago: University of Chicago Press, 1987); Lloyd I. Rudolph and Susanne Hoeber Rudolph, *Postmodern Gandhi and Other Essays: Gandhi in the World and at Home* (New Delhi: Oxford University Press, 2006); Lloyd I. Rudolph and Susanne Hoeber Rudolph, *Explaining Indian Democracy: A Fifty-Year Perspective, 1956–2006*, 3 vols (New Delhi: Oxford University Press, 2008).

4.   Lloyd I. Rudolph and Susanne Hoeber Rudolph, *Essays on Rajputana: Reflections on History, Culture and Administration* (New Delhi: Concept Publishing Company, 1984).

5.   Susanne Hoeber Rudolph and Lloyd I. Rudolph (with Mohan Singh Kanota), *Reversing the Gaze: Amar Singh's Diary–A Colonial Subject's Narrative of Imperial India* (New Delhi: Oxford University Press, 2000).

6.   Philip Woodruff, *The Men Who Ruled India* (London: Jonathan Cape, 1953); Parshotam Mehra, *A Dictionary of Modern Indian History, 1707–1947* (Delhi: Oxford University Press, 1985); Surjit Mansingh, *Historical Dictionary of India* (Lanham: Scarecrow Press, 1996).

7.   Ramya Sreenivasan, *The Many Lives of a Rajput Queen: Heroic Pasts in India, c. 1500–1900* (Seattle: University of Washington Press, 2007); Cynthia Talbot, *The Last Hindu Emperor: Prithviraj Chauhan and the Indian Past, 1200–2000* (Cambridge: Cambridge University Press, 2016).

Acknowledgments

We would like to acknowledge the care and skill Francis W. Hoeber brought to the final revision of this book. We have no doubt that his effort as an editor and historian have made the book better. We are grateful that he was able to carry this project through to completion when we could not.

Lloyd I. Rudolph
Susanne Hoeber Rudolph
Oakland, California
December 2015

PART I: ON THE WRITINGS OF COLONEL TOD

1 Writing and Reading Tod's *Rajasthan**

Interpreting the Text and Its Historiography

We first encountered Col. James Tod's *The Annals and Antiquities of Rajasthan* in Jaipur. The year was 1956. We had driven to India overland from London and were living in Bissau House as guests of the Thakur of Bissau, the late Raghubir Singh. The Ford Foundation had given us Foreign Area Training Grants to study, in the language of the time, "political development." We wondered how India had become a liberal democracy and whether it could remain one. In his 1831 visit to America, the youthful Alexis de Tocqueville had a similar question on his mind. His answer in *Democracy in America* featured associational life. Did India have an associational life? If it did, what was it like? In so poor, diverse, and hierarchal a country, could India's associational life sustain liberal democracy? Our answer in *The Modernity of Tradition* was that it could.

We had come to Jaipur, the capital of the newly formed state of Rajasthan, because Ford Foundation officers and interviewers wanted to know how we were going to study so vast and complex a place as "India." We invented an answer. We would study a state in the north and a state in the south, one from formerly British India and one from formerly Princely India. The result was that we spent six months in Rajasthan and six months in Madras (now Tamil Nadu). Which brings us back to Tod. How could we start to know Rajasthan? Our academic, administrative, and Rajput friends told us to start by reading Colonel James Tod's *The Annals and Antiquities of Rajasthan*. The well-marked hefty, khaki-bound two- volumes-in-one 1920 print of the 1914 Douglas Sladen edition shares pride of place in our bookshelves with the elegant wonderfully illustrated two volume first edition, the first volume published in 1829, the second in 1832. The *Annals* proved to be a daunting challenge, full of what at the time seemed to be arcane facts and esoteric knowledge. We have spent a good many years working on its meaning and import. What follows is in part what we learned from the text, in part, indeed a larger part, what we learned about the text and its career.

Before turning to why the text was written the way it was and to its career, we want to introduce James Tod, the author, by characterizing his life, career, and accomplishments. Next we turn to analyzing and explaining why and how he wrote *The Annals and Antiquities* the way he did. Our concluding section will examine how and with what consequences the *Annals* were read by the principal protagonists of the text, the Rajputs of Rajasthan, the warriors who ruled its ancient kingdoms; by officials, defenders, and critics of the East India Company and its successor in 1858, the Government of India; and by Indian nationalists. The result should show how Tod's *Annals* shaped Rajput, imperial, and nationalist identity and historiography. Like the story for Americans of the Puritans fleeing persecution and establishing a "city on the hill" in "the new world," Tod's story for Indians of valorous ancient Rajput kingdoms has become an origin myth.

Introducing Tod

Tod has not found a place in Philip Woodruff's "The Founders", the title of Volume 1 of Woodruff's [actually Philip Mason's] influential two-volume *The Men Who Ruled India*, a pantheon for East India officials who ruled India from Clive's victory at Plassey in 1757 until the mutiny and rebellion one hundred years later in 1857. During his 23 years (1799–1822) of arduous service to the Company he surveyed and mapped western India, the India that stretched from Saurashtra in the far west

to the Doab in central India; played a critical role in establishing British hegemony on the subcontinent by providing the
intelligence needed for victory over the Marathas in 1817; contributed to the remarkable outburst of orientalist learning associated with the Asiatic Society of Bengal by, *inter alia*,
establishing the study of numismatics in India and, most
remarkable of all, over a four-year period in Mewar (Udaipur),
gathering the materials and doing much of the research for
the *Annals*.

The 17-year-old James Tod arrived in Calcutta in 1799 to
begin service in the Company's Bengal Army. He had been
appointed a cadet on the recommendation of his well-con-
nected uncle, Patrick Heatley. Prior to his departure for
Calcutta he had attended a short training course at the Royal
Military Academy at Woolwich.[1] Apart from his limited
professional and technical training at Woolwich, little is known
about his education prior to his departure for India. His education, including the likelihood that he was something of an
autodidact, is a matter of some mystery. We are left to wonder
about his education because of his subsequent command, in
the *Annals* and *Travels*, of the literature of the Scottish enlightenment, ancient Greece and Rome, and of his own time, the
late-eighteenth and early-nineteenth centuries. His paternal
and maternal families were part of Scotland's remarkable eighteenth-century diaspora.[2] His father, James Tod, married Mary
Heatley in New York in 1779 but his son, also James, was born
in Islington, near London, on March 20, 1782. Soon after his

marriage, James senior, along with his brother John, left America for India where they became indigo planters at Mirzapur. By 1782 when young James was born, the brothers had left India. Although it seems young James grew up in England, little is known about his life as a child or where or how he was educated.

Young James had a deep and distinguished Scottish lineage. The family of his maternal grandfather, Andrew Heatley, held a landed estate in Lanarkshire for four centuries. Andrew Heatley had emigrated to Newport, Rhode Island, where he married Mary Grant, daughter of Suetonious Grant, a resident of Newport since 1725 when he had immigrated from Inverness, Scotland. Suetonious had sold the baronetcy he had inherited from his grandfather to his cousin, Alexander Grant, a successful London merchant who seems to have been the person who formally nominated young James to the East India Company cadetship that his uncle, Patrick Heatley, is said to have arranged for him.[3]

After his arrival in India, James Tod served the Company in central and western India in military, surveying, intelligence, and political capacities as it contested with the Marathas to be the successor to Mughal hegemony on the subcontinent. When in 1818 the rulers of kingdoms in Rajputana signed treaties recognizing the suzerainty of the Company, he became the Company's first political agent at Mewar. For years and at great cost to his health he camped in tents in harsh climes to tirelessly map central and western India, also collecting and preserving Rajasthan bardic literature. In his last four years (1818–22) he amassed the material and many of the ideas for his monumental work. Tod benefited greatly from access to what today is called the Saraswati Bhandar, the Maharana's personal library. He was the first historian to examine and use the library. Much of the material he deposited with the Royal Asiatic Society after his return to England, including copies of 15 Sanskrit, Hindi, and Rajasthani manuscripts frequently referred to in the *Annals*, and other valuable historical materials such as ancient coins, copper-plate grants, genealogical charts, old documents, and paintings, were given to him by Maharana Bhim Singh. Before the age of photography, his cousin Captain Waugh, who accompanied him on his tours, made the priceless sketches that, as copper plate prints, adorn the first edition of the *Annals*.

Before being driven out of India at 41 by the Company resident to the Mughal court in Delhi, David Ochterlony, Tod had played an important part in mapping, conquering, and, most important, culturally inscribing Indian space by daring and arduous feats of surveying, war, and intelligence. Forced to retire by Ochterlony's intrigues and machinations and in any case suffering from ill health, Tod returned to England in 1823.[4] Most of the writing of the *Annals* was done in London (c. 1823–31) where he served as the first Librarian of the recently founded Royal Asiatic Society. The first volume of *The Annals and Antiquities of Rajasthan* was published in 1829, the second in 1832. Tod's text took on new meaning and new life after Queen Victoria's proclamation of direct rule in 1858 and even more so in 1877 when Disraeli had Victoria declared Queen Empress of India. With direct and imperial rule India's princely rulers became pillars of support and legitimation. Tod's celebration of their ancient pedigrees and feudal status and honor became grist for the mill of imperial ideology and symbolic representation. In the imperial era his *Annals* was naturalized, treated as a foundational text, and given canonical standing.

Tod served the East India Company in India for 23 years, from his arrival in Calcutta in 1799 until 1822, the year before his departure from Bombay. In retrospect his greatest accomplishment may have been the four years he devoted while carrying out his duties as the Company's Political Agent in Mewar to mastering Mewar's language,[5] culture, and history. Tod's prodigious "field work" in Mewar was done in the face of formidable challenges to his role as Political Agent from his rival and superior in New Delhi, David Ochterlony; from Mewar's court nobles who resented and resisted his effort to "restore" the Maharana's authority and resources; and from Mewar's tribal others, the Meos of the northern march and the Bhils of the southern, who resisted Mewar's authority. It would have taken considerable discipline, energy, and imagination to meet and master these arduous challenges in the ordinary course but even more while coping, as Tod did throughout most of his career in India, with the debilitating effects of ill-health.

Readying himself to be the author of the *Annals* did not exhaust his accomplishments. Like Lewis and Clark at about the same time who provided President Jefferson with geographical knowledge of the Louisiana Territory (reaching to the Pacific Ocean from west and north of the Mississippi River), Tod, as Richard Strachey wrote in 1810,

> was engaged in collecting geographical materials, relating chiefly to the countries between the Indus [in the northwest] and Bundelkhund, the Junna and the Nerbudda [in the east and south] ... He was ever ready to communicate the information he acquired ... which, at that important period, proved most useful: it was well appreciated by Government.[6]

Tod also willy-nilly created more or less in his person the first (British) intelligence service in India, a service that proved decisive in making the Company and, via the Company, Britain the victors in the contest with the Marathas to succeed the Mughals as the hegemonic power on the Indian subcontinent. In this sense, Tod played a pivotal role in the military and political history of India.

Tod came to know the Marathas early on his career. In 1805, as a 24-year-old junior officer, he was assigned to the escort of Graeme Mercer, a friend of his uncle, Patrick Heatley, and the Company's Envoy and Resident at the court of Daulat Rao Scindia, the Maratha chief.[7] For the next eight years he remained with the escort. In 1813, the year before the onset of the Third Maratha War, Tod was promoted to Captain and put in charge of the escort. Throughout these years personally and with the aid of paid assistants he studied and surveyed the terrain, in time coining such geographic terms as "Rajasthan," "Malwa," and "Central India" and becoming increasingly familiar with the outlook and habits of leading Maratha personalities. In 1815, the map he sent the Governor-General, Lord Hastings, and his knowledge of the Maratha's "order-of-battle" created crucial strategic advantages for the Company's forces. Tod provided plans for military operations and supervised an intelligence department. The Maratha defeat in 1817 opened the way in 1818 to treaties of "subordinate cooperation" with several of the Rajput kingdoms. Tod, now 36, was appointed Political Agent to the Western Rajput States by the Governor-General.[8] His momentous four years in Mewar had begun.

Tod's final accomplishment was as a scholar-administrator. He lived and worked at what he felt to be the periphery of the East India Company's world in India. Although a member of the Asiatic Society located in distant Calcutta, the seat of the East India Company's Governor-General and his administration, he was sufficiently awed by the scholar-administrator members resident there and sufficiently unsure of how to present and interpret the massive amount of material he had gathered that he refrained from submitting his work for publication in *Asiatic Researches*, much less beginning a general work on Rajasthan.[9] It was only after his return to England in 1823 and becoming the first Librarian of the newly formed Royal Asiatic Society in

1824 that he began to publish articles based on the extensive material he had gathered and on his views about India's civilization.

Among the first was an article in the first volume of the *Transactions* of the Royal Asiatic Society on ancient coins. O.P. Kejariwal credits Tod as being "the first person to have taken a scholarly interest in ancient coins ... His article ... evoked wide interest. The discovery of a large number of Roman and Bactrian coins in India made it obvious that a study of coins in India would contribute to the study of ancient Europe."[10] John Keay also describes Tod as "the person who launched Indian numismatics."[11] Apart from this pioneering numismatic work, Tod helped to launch the study of ancient Indian history. In 1822, during his "travels in western India," he "discovered" and took copies of two short sections from what came to be called the Girnar Rock Edict, "the memorial," as Tod put it at the time of his discovery, "of some great conqueror." That great conqueror proved to be Ashoka. Tod could not read the script but after James Prinsep deciphered it Tod's copies proved to be critical in establishing that Ashoka's edicts spanned a subcontinental empire.

In concluding our thoughts on James Tod, the person, we ask ourselves a question that has, after Edward Said's influential book *Orientalism*,[12] Michel Foucault's various observations about the relationship of knowledge and power, and, for India particularly, Ronald Inden's *Imagining India*,[13] become *de rigueur*: why did Tod pursue knowledge, why did he map central and western India, why did he write *The Annals and Antiquities of Rajasthan?* How should we interpret and theorize his motives and text?

However much Tod's mapping and intelligence work contributed to the Company's victory over the Marathas in 1817 and however much his work from 1818 to 1822 as Political Agent in Mewar contributed to the consolidation of British power on the Indian subcontinent, did he write the *Annals*, as the Edward Said of *Orientalism* would have us believe, because in colonial contexts knowledge necessarily serves power? As Foucault would have it, Tod was in the grip of power; willy-nilly he did what power required of him. One way or another, what he knows and why and how he knows is determined by his colonial location.

We find such strong claims for structural determination excessive because they too radically discount agency and the related mentalities, tropes, and epistemes, to be examined later, that shaped Tod's thinking, choices, and actions. One of the reasons Tod wrote the *Annals* in the first place and wrote it the way he did was his engagement with what might be called the original and authentic "orientalists," the persons associated with Sir William Jones and his protector, Governor-General Warren Hastings. Did the stellar cast of scholar-administrators who populated the Asiatic Society[14] and who created an amazing body of Indological knowledge pursue knowledge because they were pursuing power or because of their love of learning and intellectual curiosity? Must we choose one or the other?

Our reading of James Tod and of the other Asiatic Society orientalists gives considerable weight to love of learning and intellectual curiosity.

As a teenage undergraduate at Oxford, William Jones mastered not only several European languages but also took up Arabic and Persian, languages in his view of two great civilizations. Years later, as he approached India by sea, he thought of those civilizations, one to the north and one to the south of the route his ship was taking. His trope was "civilization." After he mastered Sanskrit in India he declared it and its literature at least the equal of Greek and its literature. Like Tod, Jones and his Asiatic Society colleagues sought for parallels between Indian, Greek, and Roman civilizations. It was an era that saw the world in terms of civilizations and that anticipated civilizational progress.[15]

Writing the *Annals*

We turn from Tod the man to Tod the author. What paradigms and concepts, tropes and metaphors, assumptions and tacit knowledge, did he bring to the writing of the *Annals*? Why and how did he write the *Annals* the way he did? We read the *Annals* not only as a work of positive scholarship about history and ethnography and legend and myth but also as a text which can be explicated as intellectual history. In this chapter we identify and analyze authors and ideas, the mental constructs, that Tod brought to bear on the selection and interpretation of the massive evidence he so assiduously and meticulously compiled.[16]

We find that his interpretation was animated by three related metaphors or models—medieval feudalism, romantic nationalism, and civilizational progress. The most conspicuous influence on the writing of the *Annals* is Henry Hallam's *Middle Ages*.[17] First published in 1818, various editions of Hallam's work shaped perceptions and historiography in Britain, France, and the United States for most of the nineteenth century. References to it dominate the five chapters of the framing section of Volume I, "Sketch of a Feudal System in Rajasthan."

In the opening pages of these generative chapters, written we imagine circa 1828 when he is finishing the first volume of the *Annals*, we read,

> ... many years have passed since I first entertained these opinions [that the Rajpoot states martial system is analogous to the ancient feudal system of Europe], long before [1818 when] ... any connection existed between these states and the British government; when their geography [which Tod did so much to establish] was little known to us, and their history still less so [again, Tod makes it known]. At that period I frequently travelled amongst them for amusement, making these objects [e.g. geography and history] subservient thereto, and laying the result freely before my government.

Tod then treats directly with the authors that shaped his world view:

> I had abundant sources of intelligence to guide me in forming my analogies: Montesquieu, Hume, Millar, Gibbon; but I sought only general resemblances and lineaments similar to those before me.[18]

He then reveals the decisive source for reading Rajasthan texts and archives; oral and written bardic literature; and rituals and politics of Mewar court society—in the light of medieval feudalism.

> A more perfect source, because more familiar picture, has since appeared [in 1818] by an author [here he footnotes "Hallam's *Middle Ages*"], who has drawn aside the veil of mystery which covered the subject, owing to its being till then but imperfectly understood. I compared the features of Rajpoot society with the finished picture of this eloquent writer, and shall be satisfied with having substantiated the claim of these tribes to participation in a system, hitherto deemed to belong exclusively to Europe. I am aware, of the danger of hypothesis, and shall advance nothing that I do not accompany by incontestable proofs.[19]

Tod's Scottish ancestry played a crucial role in his romantic turn to feudalism and classicism. Byron, for example, was from Scotland, a country with powerful links to late eighteenth-century and early nineteenth-century Romanticism. Indeed, Byron was very much on Tod's mind both as a poet and, as we shall see later, a fellow activist in support of Greek nationalism. In Chapter XXX of Volume 1 on Ajmer, Tod reports his first sight of "the [Chauhan] castle of Manika Rae [at Ajmer] where the first Rajpoot blood which the arms of conversion shed" summoned up an image for him from Byron's *Childe Harold*:

> There was a day when they were young and proud,
> Banners on high, and battles passed below;
> But they who fought are in a bloody shroud,
> And those which wave are shredless dust ere now,
> And the bleak battlements shall bear no future blow.[20]

Scottish too was Sir Walter Scott, "the herald of the medieval revival ... and the inventor of a fictitious sentimental national tradition ..."[21] Scottish Enlightenment luminaries such as David Hume, Adam Smith, John Millar, and Edward Gibbon, who was "for all intents and purposes ... intellectually a Scot,"[22] shaped Tod's historical understanding, including his view of stages in the course of realizing "civilization."[23] Starting with *Waverly* set in the Highlands in 1814 and more or less ending with *The Surgeon's Daughter* set in India in 1827, Scott spread Romanticism by inventing the historical novel and with it the mass market for novels, a market which English novelists such as Jane Austen, Charles Dickens, William Thackeray, George Eliot, Anthony Trollope, and continental novelists such as Balzac, Hugo, Flaubert, and Tolstoy were the beneficiaries. The historical novel was a new art form that paved the way for Tod's *Annals* by imagining difference and embracing the other. An "intriguing blend of imaginative fantasy and meticulous fidelity to historical truth," it celebrated "emotional loyalties rather than economic calculation [and] ... heroic self-sacrifice rather than rational self-interest."[24] In this way Scott introduced a key ingredient in modern consciousness, "a sense of historical detachment," something that Macaulay[25] and other utilitarian and evangelical early Victorians lacked but something that enabled Tod to imagine and, to an extent, be the Rajput other.

The Annals and Antiquities of Rajasthan was written and published for a reading public whose tastes and sensibilities had been shaped by several generations of "romantic" authors.[26] Repudiating eighteenth-century Enlightenment rationalism and market commercialism the Romantics celebrated nature, sentiment, the picturesque, and the exotic and sometimes erotic other. Romantics like Byron, but also Shelley, are particularly important because, in an era when East India Company trade, conquest, and politics were center stage in the drama of English public life, the extravagant orientalism of their literary productions about India catered to a burgeoning public demand.[27] In May 1813 Byron urged the Irish poet Tom Moore

> to join him on the bandwagon of "oriental" poetry: "Stick to the East"—the oracle Stael [Madame De Stael] told me it was the only poetical policy ... The little I have done in that way is merely a "voice in the wilderness" for you; and, if it has had any success, that also will prove that the public are orientalizing, and pave the path for you.[28]

Tod's own romanticism is epitomized in our view by his attitude toward heroic death, particularly heroic youthful death. To die in battle fighting gallantly for a noble cause may have been the highest form of glory for a feudal knight. To die young in battle was even more glorious. Youth was the apogee of life; after the bloom of youth came decay then death. These perceptions and attitudes are captured in Tod's account of the death of the 16-year-old Putta of Kelwa in 1568 when a Mughal army under Akbar's command sacked Chitor, symbol of the Rajput's code of honor:

But the names which shine brightest in the gloomy page of the annals of Mewar, which are still held sacred by the bard and the true Rajpoot, and immortalised by Akbar's own pen, are Jeimul of Bednore and Putta of Kailwa ... When Saloombra[29] fell at the gate of the sun, the command devolved on Putta of Kelwa. He was only sixteen: his father had fallen in the first shock, and his mother had survived but to rear the sole heir of the house. Like the Spartan mother of old, she commanded him to put on the "safron robe," and to die for Cheetore: but surpassing the Greecian dame, she illustrated her percept by example; and lest any soft "compunctious visitings" ... might dim the lustre of Kailwa, she armed the young bride [of her son] with a lance, with her descended the rock, and the defenders of Cheetore saw her fall, fighting by the side of her Amazonian mother ... Jeimul took the lead on the fall of the kin of Mewar ... He saw there was no ultimate hope of salvation, the northern defences being entirely destroyed, and he resolved to

signalize the end of his career. The fatal Johur was commanded, while eight thousand Rajpoots ate the last "beera"
[pan; according to Tod without opium] together and put on
their saffron robes; the gates were thrown open, the work of
destruction commenced, and few survived "to stain the
yellow mantle" by inglorious surrender.[30]

Tod's romanticism in the *Annals* emerged in the shadow of
a struggle over British policy in India. The struggle took the
form of a clash of civilizational understandings. Were the
Rajput kingdoms to be alien and conquered peoples who paid
tribute to swell the coffers of the Company or were they to be
respected and trusted allies who shared a common interest in
the security and welfare of the Indian subcontinent? More
broadly, were Indians, as Kipling three generations later would
have it, "lesser breeds without the law" for whom British rulers
were called upon to assume "the white man's burden" to civilize? Or were they the bearers of an ancient civilization who
should be cultivated as worthy allies?

Tod's differences with David Ochterlony over how to treat
Mewar and other Rajput kingdoms[31] foreshadowed even more
profound philosophical differences with James Mill. In prepa-
ration for what became the Company's new charter in 1834,
both gave parliamentary testimony that addressed the theory
and practice of British rule in India. Mill's testimony reflected
the views propounded in his six-volume *The History of British
India*. It had first appeared in 1817 but remained, until the
Company's demise in 1857, the Company's *de facto* official

text. Tod's testimony was consistent with the views propounded in his *Annals*, the second volume of which was published in the same year that he provided parliamentary testimony, 1832. Mill spoke as a "liberal" utilitarian, Tod as a romantic conservative.[32]

Mill's "liberal" utilitarianism tended to deny difference in the name of a commitment to universal truth. It was an axiom about human nature, for example, that persons maximized pleasure and minimized pain and an axiom of public policy to seek the greatest happiness of the greatest number. Such truths are independent of time, place, and circumstance. They determine human consciousness, preferences, and actions everywhere and always. In pursuit of sameness and uniformity, Mill's utilitarian universalism could also lead to policies and actions designed to destroy rather than to deny difference, to conversions of idolaters rather than to legislation designed to civilize the other so that they become like us.

Tod's romantic conservatism tends to respect the other, to sympathize, even to empathize with difference as it appears in diverse forms of life. Tod respects, admires, and even identifies with the Rajput other. Ultimately, in a distant future, he imagines that a hypothesized common Scythian origin of Britons and Rajputs and civilizational progress will enable Britons and Rajputs to realize a common brotherhood. Mill's and Tod's parliamentary testimonies in 1832, like their respective major works, reflect respectively what Uday Singh Mehta, in *Liberalism and Empire*, represents as a Lockean view of human sameness and a Burkean view of human diversity.[33] Mill's and Tod's opposed perspectives on the meaning and consequences of differences in culture and religion, world view and way of life, not only animated the ideological debate in the formative years of colonialism in India but also foreshadowed today's debate about whether civilizations can live in concord or must clash.

Tod and Nationalism

Tod wrote not only under the spell of Henry Hallam's medievalism and Scottish romanticism but also at the opening phase of modern nationalism. As indicated already by his invocation of Greek parallels in the Putta story cited above and, more generally, frequent allusions to events and symbols of ancient Greece, Tod's writing was deeply influenced by its "classical" civilization. In 1821, what was believed to be ancient Greece's contemporary expression, a Hellenic Greek nation, began a struggle for "national liberty" against the "despotic" rule of the Ottoman Turks. This riveted attention in Europe and America on a people imagined by Adamantios Koraes from his Paris exile as "Hellenes," a nation descended from the "classical" Greeks of Sparta and Athens, and thus the fountainhead and inspiration of European civilization.[34] It was their freedom struggle with which Tod identified and that shaped the writing of the *Annals*. As Nigel Leask makes clear in *British Romantic Writers and the East; Anxieties of Empire*, romantic poets such as

Byron and Shelley were not only passionately philhellenic but also passionately orientalist.[35] With the outbreak of the Greek war for independence in 1821 Shelly wrote: "We are all Greeks. Our laws, our literature, our religion, our arts all have their roots in Greece."[36] Tod's narrative of Mewar's struggle against the Mughal Empire resembles his perception of the Greek struggle against the Ottoman Turks; Rana Pratap's near victory over the Mughals at the battle of Haldighati [1576] is likened to Sparta's resistance against overwhelming Persian force at Thermopylae.

Norbert Peabody has shown how Tod's *Annals* introduced the discourse of the "nation" by analyzing and explaining differences between Rajputs and Marathas and alluding to territorialized cultural boundaries separating them. Tod was not being anachronistic in his use of terms such as nation and nationalism. These terms were already being used during the Napoleonic wars by the British with respect to the rest of Europe. The future East India Company Governor-General, Lord Bentinck [1828–33], captured this paradoxical relationship epigrammatically when, upon his arrival in Palermo in 1811, he is said to have remarked, "Bonaparte makes kings; England makes nations."[37]

Years ago when we first began writing about Tod's mentality we could only surmise that his thinking was deeply affected by the opening phases of nationalism in Europe. We wondered whether the Greek freedom struggle against the Ottoman Turks that riveted European (and American) attention when it "began" in 1821 had come to Tod's attention in what, from a European perspective, was a remote corner of India, Mewar. The struggle was depicted as an effort by a "nation" imagined as "Hellenes," descendants of the ancient Greeks and perceived as inventors of European civilization, to liberate themselves from the Ottoman Turks' "despotism." We had inferred that Tod might have modelled his account of Mewar's freedom struggle against the might of Akbar's Mughal Empire on the Hellenic Greek's struggle against the Ottoman Turks but couldn't substantiate it. Was it at best an elective affinity?

We believe that an essay with the title "Greece in 1823 and 1824 by the Honourable Colonel Leicester Stanhope," published anonymously in volume 3, no. 11, November 1824 of *The Oriental Herald*, reflects Tod's views and may have been written by him. *The Oriental Herald* began publication in January 1824 under the editorship of James Silk Buckingham. Both Buckingham and Tod were expelled from India in 1823, Buckingham from Calcutta, Tod from Udaipur, for opposing Company policies and persons. The editorial stance of Buckingham's *Calcutta Journal* was to advocate the abolition of the Company's monopoly and the suppression of its political power. Tod had opposed David Ochterlony's efforts to extract maximum tribute from Mewar and other Rajput kingdoms and to treat their rulers as oriental despots. Tod sympathized and empathized with Rajasthan's Rajput rulers and thought Britain should respect their civilization and treat them as friends and allies.[38] In the words of his dedication to George IV in the first volume of the *Annals* (1829),

> The Rajpoot princes, happily rescued, by the triumph of the British arms, from the yoke of lawless oppression, are now the most remote tributaries to Your Majesty's extensive empire; and their admirer and annalist may, perhaps, be permitted to hope, that the sighs of this ancient and interesting race for the restoration of their former independence, which it would suit our wisest policy to grant, may be deemed not undeserving of Your Majesty's regard.

There is some evidence, not conclusive, that Tod wrote "Greece in 1823 and 1824" which reviews Col. Leicester Stanhope's book of the same name, after he arrived in England from India in April 1823.

But even if Tod did not write "Greece," we believe the essays reflect his values and perspective. We have not found evidence that Tod and Buckingham knew each other but even if they did not know each other it seems clear that they shared oppositionist views about Company rule in India and the importance and value of public opinion and of "national liberty." They also shared ties to Col. Leicester Stanhope, whose book about his experiences in Greece was reviewed in the "Greece" essay. We know, for example, from army lists for the Third Anglo-Maratha War, a war, as we have seen, in which Tod's intelligence operation played a vital role, that the Cavalry

Brigade of the Gujarat Division of the army of the Deccan was commanded by Lt. Col. the Hon'ble L. Stanhope. It seems highly probable that Tod and Stanhope knew each other in India, a relationship which supports the possibility that Tod wrote the "Greece" essay reviewing Stanhope's book.

It is also possible that James Silk Buckingham, a prolific writer and an intrepid editor, wrote the essay. Whether Tod or Buckingham wrote it, however, we feel confident that the essay on "Greece" provides strong evidence of Tod's deep knowledge of and identification with the 1821 "Hellenic" Greek rebellion against Ottoman rule. Here is some of the language from the opening paragraphs of that essay:

> The glorious revolutions of Greece has strongly attracted the attention of all liberal men, to whom it had long appeared surprising that that classic land, the very birth-place and cradle of liberty, should have remained during so many centuries under the yoke of foreign tyrants ... in every corner of Europe, this glorious result of the struggle excited the warmest admiration, and in almost every country the spirit of the people was roused to participation in so noble a cause ... In Switzerland, in Germany, and even in Russia, committees have been organized to assist in the regeneration of Grecian liberty, and a portion at least of the English people followed speedily the example which had been set before them by others. Assisted by the contributions of this part of the British public, the Greek Committee of London, at the head of which were many noble and respected names,

exerted itself with success in forwarding the progress of Grecian liberty and independence. ... [The Honorable Colonel Leicester Stanhope] offered his services to proceed to Greece as agent of the Committee ... and he soon departed from London with full powers ... to act, on his arrival in Greece, in conjunction with Lord Byron for the advancement of the cause in which they had both so zealously embarked.

We find echoes of this memoir in Tod's *Annals* where he tells us that Mewar's battle with the Mughals at Haldighati in 1576 is like the Spartans' battle at Thermopylae with the Persians. Thus by using the Hellenic Greek's struggle for freedom and independence against the Ottoman Turks to construct Mewar's against the Mughals, he assimilates both to a classical paradigm, Sparta's defense of Greek freedom against a Persian other.

Reading the *Annals*

In the naturalized categories of official Raj ethnography, an ethnography that Princely India came to share, Rajasthan's kingdoms were ruled by Rajputs. The term "Rajput" encompassed both kshatriya and aristocratic status, both the warrior-ruler *varna* of India's ancient texts[39] and the landed nobility and gentry familiar to English discourse. British discourse about "caste" conflated not only *jāti* and *varna* but also culture

and biology; genetic codes determined character and status.[40]
Jats were by nature cultivators; Rajputs by nature rulers and
warriors. In nineteenth-century readings, to be a Rajput was a
condition outside history, essential and timeless.

From at least Mughal times Rajput identity has been
shaped by the oral and written panegyrics of court bards.
Ironically, in the late nineteenth century, Rajasthan's paramount bardic authority had become Col. James Tod's *The
Annals and Antiquities of Rajasthan*. Published in 1829 and 1832,
his two volumes had become not only the authoritative version of bardic literature but also the dominant historiography
for Raj and Princely India. As Tod's reputation and standing
grew in the second half of the nineteenth century, it became
difficult to distinguish the local bardic traditions from the
import.

After 1857, in the post-mutiny and rebellion world of
direct rule in British India and paramountcy in Princely India,
Tod's *Annals* dominated in quite different ways both Raj and
Indian nationalist historiography. First of all, Tod's historiography not only reflected but also contributed to a burgeoning
feudal medievalism and to a revival of "classical" Hellenism
that gripped Raj consciousness and practice in the second half
of the nineteenth century.[41] For the post-Mutiny Raj in need of
an ideology to legitimate direct rule, Tod's account of
Rajputana's ancient dynasties, feudal kingdoms, and chivalric
honor fuelled the construction of the princes as loyal vassals of
the crown. In 1876, for example, Disraeli agreed with Queen

Victoria's controversial request to be styled Empress of India.[42] Lord Lytton, the viceroy, used the momentous occasion to orchestrate a Mughal-style durbar at Delhi in January 1877. Victoria was declared Empress of India, India's princes, not least among them Rajput rulers, acknowledged her rule and declared their loyalty. The princes in turn were accorded pride of place in a new imperial cosmology that recognized them as India's "natural leaders," as Lord Curzon called them. The princes' loyalty and deference to the British crown in the person of Queen Victoria were counted on to legitimize, support, and secure British rule in India. Tod would no doubt have disapproved of this culmination because it made clear that Rajput rulers had become what his hopes and policy were directed to avoid, dependents and subordinates of the British. At the same time he would have approved, we believe, the medievalism and orientalism of the occasion.

After 1857, Tod's account of the chivalric Rajput also opened the way for an imperial theory of martial races.[43] In 1857, the year of the mutiny and rebellion, the largely brahman Bengal Army had proved disloyal and treacherous. Tod both naturalized and historicized a warrior-ruler ideal by celebrating 1,000 years of Rajput bravery and valor. In the years after the mutiny and rebellion it proved expedient to construct an ideology of martial ("masculine") and non- martial ("effeminate") races. Rajputs served as the prototype of the martial races. From Lord Roberts' reconstruction of a post-Mutiny Indian Army on "racial" lines[44] to Lt. General Sir George MacMunn's

The Martial Races of India (1932),[45] Tod's Rajputs served to valorize a racial theory of fighting men. While accepting Sir William Jones' theory of Indo-European languages and peoples, Tod differed from Jones' brahman-centric view by holding that Rajputs and Britons shared a common ancestry as descendants of an ancient Scythian people whose empire was thought to have been located in and around the Caucasus region of Central Asia.[46] The legitimacy of British rule in India and subcontinental security in the era of the "Great Game" in Asia came to rely on co-opting, rewarding, and celebrating these "martial races."[47]

Different from this colonial reading, Indian nationalists, starting with those in Bengal, brought a different interest to their reading of Tod. Tod's accounts of Rajput kings and heroes, particularly of the legendary Mewar ruler, Rana Pratap (1572–97), featured his resistance to the blandishments and power of the Mughal Empire. At Haldighati (1576) Rana Pratap almost defeated the emperor Akbar's mighty army. For twenty arduous years Pratap's guerrilla warfare held Mughal power at bay. Tod's bardic-inspired accounts of Pratap's fight to preserve Mewar's independence and honor inspired nationalist plays, poems, and histories about India's first "freedom fighter" against imperial rule.[48]

Gandhi's use of Tod was capped by his invocation of him to convince participants at the momentous Second Round Table Conference in London in 1931 that India was capable of defending itself:

There is all the material there ... Mohammedans ... Sikhs
... the Gurkha. ... Then there are the Rajputs, who are
supposed to be responsible for a thousand Thermopylaes,
and not one little Thermopylae. ... That is what the
Englishman, Colonel Tod, told us. Colonel Tod has
taught us to believe that every pass in Rajputana is a
Thermopylae. Do these people stand in need of learning
the art of defense?[49]

Tod's framing of Mewar's struggle to preserve its freedom
had an enduring impact. Fifty years later, in 1879, the romance
of the ancient, freedom-loving Rajputs was still alive and well
in Sir Alfred Lyall's authoritative historical note to the first
Gazetteer of Rajputana. Lyall wrote:

We may describe Rajputana as the region within which the
pure- blooded Rajput States have maintained their
independence under their own chieftains, and have kept
together their primitive[50] societies ever since their principal
dynasties in Northern India were cast down and swept away
by the Mussalman irruption. Of the States of Rajputana,
eighteen belong to the first rank in the Empire, being under
treaty with the Imperial Government.[51]

By 1928, when Sir Walter Lawrence, the viceroy Lord
Curzon's private secretary, published his memoirs, *The India
We Served*, the myth of the noble Rajputs had reached its
apogee. Lawrence uses a facsimile of Rudyard Kipling's handwritten letter as the preface to his book; it refers to Lawrence's

book as a "fairytale," a book that captures the timeless India of Kipling's imperial imagination. For Lawrence,

> The highest type [of Indian] with which I am acquainted ... is the Rajput of Rajputana. ... I like to think that the ... Indians of ancient times ... resembled closely the fine thoroughbred men now living in Rajputana—whether they be called Kshattriyas ... or Aryans ... still always great and chivalrous gentlemen, with whom it is a privilege and an education to associate.[52]

These cultural enthusiasms and panegyrics, which fit well into late nineteenth-century imperial *mise-en-scène*, have been overtaken by recent critiques of Rajput historiography and identity.[53] Dirk Kolff's historical unpacking of the term "Rajput" in the sixteenth and seventeenth centuries reveals a variety of possibilities for Rajput identity and status. Kolff, for example, argues that before Mughal rule in the seventeenth century, "Rajput" was not a closed status category. The pre-Mughal term "Rajput" referred to persons with multiple identities—for example, place and sect—only one of which was that of a fighting man. Pre-Mughal Rajputs, Kolff tells us, were recruited from village-based military labor markets structured by the agricultural production cycle. The aristocratic Rajput of ancient lineage, Kolff argues, is a creature of the seventeenth and eighteenth centuries when, under the influence of the Mughal court culture, "something like a new Rajput Great Tradition" takes shape.[54] Raj officials after 1858 willingly endorsed the Rajput Great Tradition story, a story that justified placing Rajput princes at the center of the imperial ensemble as loyal but independent feudatories. It was an arrangement that suited the often socially ambitious British middle class members of the Indian Civil Service eager for deference from the exotic princes and aristocrats with whom they hobnobbed and from whom they expected compliance.[55]

Indeed, during the great revolt in 1857 against British rule most of Rajputana's princes sided with the British.[56] Their help in a time of peril ushered in an era of mutual appreciation and support that lasted till independence in 1947. After 1857 the Raj relied increasingly on Princely India as a source of legitimacy and political support. The princes in turn came to rely on British recognition and power to legitimize and secure their rule.

Amar Singh's Diary

We conclude by invoking the Rajput we know best, the diarist Amar Singh.[57] Particularly in the early years of his diary, he often explored the meaning and consequences of his Rajput identity. His lineage roots are found in the Champawat Rathores from Jodhpur, his status rests on a title and estate of an influential service family in Jaipur, and his education and early career were shaped by an influential patron, the celebrated Sir Pratap Singh, for 22 years the Prince Regent of Jodhpur. Sir Pratap's prominence in the *fin-de-siècle* imperial great chain of being makes opportunities available to Amar Singh in Princely and British India. Amar Singh initially knows himself from stories about Rajputs that he has heard or read. In September 1898, under the urging of his respected teacher, Barath Ram Nathji, he begins writing his diary, an activity that he continues for 44 years until his death on November 1, 1942. He learns about Rajput valor and honor, about Rajputs' contributions to the making and maintaining of the Mughal Empire, about Rana Pratap's resistance to Mughal rule and struggle to maintain Mewar's independence, about Rajput pride of place in the British Raj. The stories he hears about who and what a Rajput is are fed by Col. James Tod's romantic Eurocentric historiography and neo-bardic, feudal construction of the martial Rajput.

But there is another side to his Rajput identity. Like Mohandas Gandhi's self-critical and radically reformist commitment to his Hindu identity, Amar Singh's commitment to his Rajput identity is reflexive and self-critical. He knows Rajput ideals, what Rajputs at their best can and should be, but his diary entries are replete with spirited accounts of Rajputs behaving wrongly and badly. Indeed, again like Gandhi, he is familiar with, indeed he often empathizes with the standards and outlook of the imperial British other. He lives liminally, on the border between Princely and British India. He is among the first to serve as a King's Commissioned Officer in the British Indian Army. After his retirement from the Indian Army in 1922, the 44-year-old Amar Singh returns to Jaipur where he is asked to raise the Jaipur Lancers and becomes something of a guide and mentor to the new Maharaja, the 12-year-old Man Singh. In time he becomes Commander of the Jaipur State Forces. His Rajputness is continuously on trial not only in a public sphere shared with the British but also in the private sphere of extended family life in a 100-person *havelī*. His reflexivity takes the form of inner and outer critiques of who and what the Rajputs have become and should be.

Amar Singh dies in November 1942. Five years later, soon after the close of World War II, India gains independence but the country is partitioned into successor states. Less noticed but of great significance for Rajput identity and history, the princely states, including 22 in the Rajputana agency, were "integrated" into the Indian Union. The princes lost what sovereignty they had under "paramountcy,"[58] a relationship of "subordinate cooperation" with the British crown, when they "acceded" to the newly formed Government of India. India's old regime had begun to crumble. The princely states of Rajasthan were merged into a newly formed state of India's federal system without a shot being fired. The first state election in 1952 under a universal franchise almost returned a Rajput-led government but its potential leader, the Maharaja of Jodhpur, Hanut Singh, an inveterate and intrepid flier, died in a plane crash as the polls closed thereby depriving the princely and feudal order of a potential one seat majority and, more importantly, its leader. In the event leaders of the States' Peoples' Freedom Movement, Jai Narayan Vyas of Jodhpur,

Manickulal Verma of Udaipur, and Hiralal Shastri of Jaipur, who had led their organizations into a newly formed state unit of the Nehru-led Congress Party, formed Rajasthan's first democratically elected government.

The new government's first order of business was "land reform," a euphemism in Rajasthan for "*jāgīr* resumption." It removed, with compensation, Rajput aristocrats from their revenue-bearing landed estates. It also ousted their *chhote bhā'īs*, younger brothers, from their small holdings. Dismissed from service with maharajas' or *jāgīrdārs'* courts and bureaucracies, they now found themselves without jobs and income. There was violence as their tenants, often Jats, forcibly occupied "resumed" lands that their younger brothers claimed as *khud-kāsht* (self-cultivation) and refused to relinquish. In a civil war of sorts between lesser Rajputs and their erstwhile tenants hundreds of policeman lost their lives while trying to maintain law and order.[59] By 1956, when a large contingent of satisfied big Rajput *jāgīrdārs* crossed the aisle to join the Mohan Lal Sukhadia-led Congress government, the old regime as such disappeared in the merger. Rajputs now tended to join other castes and classes in the competition for power, status, and benefits that had begun to characterize India's democratic politics.

Looking back nearly 60 years from the vantage point of a new century since the days when we first encountered Tod's *Annals* while living in Jaipur at Bissau House, we ask, what is left of Rajasthan's feudal society and ideology, of the image of heroism and honor summoned up by mounted warriors defending great castles from invading foes? Tod's Rajasthan is being replicated for tourists. More tourists visit Rajasthan than any other state. Its arts and crafts; its folk culture and performance arts; its fairs and fetes; its colorful clothing, turbans, and jewelry; its camels and elephants; all contribute to Rajasthan's appeal. Topping all of Rajasthan's attraction is its Rajput heritage, a heritage of princes and noblemen, their palaces and forts, castles and mansions.

Mohan Singh Kanota, our friend and co-author, was instrumental in organizing a Heritage Hotel association among Rajput princes and noblemen. The association helps Rajputs with palaces, forts, and castles to preserve their patrimony while earning an income. They do so by reproducing for tourists from home and abroad versions of Tod's Rajasthan. A thin and easily breached line separates preservation and its effort to be authentic and replication epitomized by theme parks, a form of representation that has spread from America to Europe and Japan.[60] The preservation of the great forts at Chitor, Kumbalghar, Jodhpur, Jaiselmer, and Amber and of hundreds of lesser forts, castles, palaces, and *havelīs* gives us hope that something of Tod's Rajasthan, itself a partially imagined place, can help Rajasthanis and those who visit Rajasthan to participate in the production and reproduction of Rajasthan.

Notes

*   This chapter was previously published in a similar form in Joseph Gammons and Om Prakash (eds.), *Circumambulations in South Asian History: Essays in Honour of Dirk H. A. Kolf* (Leiden; Boston: Brill, 2003). Reprinted by permission.

1.   For the early history of East India Company training institutions and their effect on knowledge about and perceptions of India, see B.S. Cohn, "Recruitment and Training of British Civil Servants in India, 1600–1860," in Ralph Braibanti (ed.), *Asian Bureaucratic Systems Emergent from the Imperial Tradition* (Durham NC: Duke University Commonwealth Studies Center, 1966).

2.   The Scottish diaspora is extensively dealt with in Arthur Herman's *How the Scots Invented the Modern World* (New York: Crown Publishers, 2001). See particularly the six chapters of Part II: "Diaspora."

3.   Biographical information about James Tod has been gleaned from a variety of sources. Most useful for biographical information— and for framing and interpretative questions—is Jason Freitag, *Serving Empire, Serving Nation: James Tod and the Rajputs of Rajasthan* (Leiden; Boston: Brill, 2009). It has put Tod scholarship on a new plane. Other sources for biographical information about Tod include his principal works: *The Annals and Antiquities of Rajasthan* (particularly William Crooke's introduction to his London 1920 edition) and *Travels in Western India* (Delhi: Oriental Publishers, 1971) whose anonymously authored "Memoir of the Author" provides something of a biography. See also G. Smith (ed.), *The Dictionary of National Biography* (London, 1960; 1912 edition by Leslie Stephen and Sidney Lee); and

Henry Cousens, "The Late Lieutenant-Colonel James Tod", *Archaeological Survey of India* (1907–8).

4.   Tod left India in broken health and defeated. Twelve years as a surveyor often spent "in camp ... subject to the inclemencies of all weather under canvas" contributed to "... the very bad state of my health" (R.H. Phillimore, *Historical Records of the Survey of India, Vol. II: 1800 to 1815*, Dehra Dun, 1950, p. 446). In 1822, at the age of 41, Tod had been forced to retire from East India Company service and leave India for England as a result of conflicts with his administrative superior, Major-General David Ochterlony (1803, Resident at the Mughal emperor's court; victorious commander in wars in Mysore and Nepal and against the Marathas, Gurkhas, and Pindaris; 1818, Resident in Rajputana when he negotiated treaties with several Rajput states; Resident again in Delhi when Tod was agent in Mewar). Ochterloney's views, policies, and actions epito- mized the kind of activist interventionism that led in time to the mutiny and rebellion of 1857. Tod, by contrast, anticipated the post- Mutiny policy of respecting the princes and relying on them as loyal feudatories of the Crown. Ochterlony was a colorful and forceful figure who played a major military and administrative role in extend- ing Company power in northern India and Nepal and whose career and despatches helped to shape pre-1857 British perceptions of and attitudes toward India. Ochterlony, who lived like a Nawab with a retinue of wives and attendants, thought he knew Indian character, languages, and manners better than Tod. Having negotiated the 1818 treaties, he found Tod's objections to Company imposed financial burden on Rajput states unwarranted and insubordinate. Ochterlony's detractors charged that he "constantly interfered in the internal

affairs of princely states," adding to the confusion. In 1825 Ochterlony chose to resign rather than suffer a "repudiation of his policy." His "papers" give us a detailed account of the conflict between Ochterlony and Tod (N.K. Sinha and A.K. Das [eds.], *Selections from the Ochterlony Papers 1818–25 in the National Archives of India* [Calcutta, 1964]). In the post-Mutiny India of direct rule, Tod's *The Annals and Antiquities of Rajasthan*, rather than Ochterlony's despatches, shaped perceptions, ideology, and historiography.

5. In a private communication Dr Rima Hooja, a prodigious scholar of Indian and Rajasthani subjects, and author of A *History of Rajasthan* (New Delhi: Rupa & Co., 2006), informs us on the basis of a letter in the "Hardwicke Papers" (Add 9868 of British Library Western Mss Collection) signed by Tod to Col. Colin McKenzie dated February 19, 1821, that Tod "extracted the Essence ... of many works in *prose and verse*, in all dialects—From the 'Deo Banee' [the Sanskrit], so called by pre-eminence—the language of the Gods, to the uncouth Basha, the Doric of Medpat or the honied words of Brij. My tutor is an adept in every one. The Suruswutti—of which is the Punjabi,—the Magadi [Behar], Guzeratti &c &c, and I understand the Rangra and blunder thro' all."

6. Tod, *Travels*, p. xxiii.

7. The Marquis of Wellesley's (Arthur Wellesley) victories in 1803 at Assaye over the Maratha Peshwa, Baji Rao II, and over Daulat Rao Sindhia, in the so-called First Maratha War, led to the signing of the Treaty of Bassein. It gave the Company effective control over the Maratha homeland by means, *inter alia*, of a military escort being stationed at the Maratha's moveable court. For summary treatment of the First Maratha War and, more generally, the Maratha era see Surjit

Mansingh, *Historical Dictionary of India* (New Delhi, 1998), pp. 57; 250–2. For summary treatments of the First, Second, and Third "Anglo-Maratha" Wars and short accounts of the Maratha chiefs involved in them (Balaji Baji Rao and Baji Rao II), see Parshotam Mehra, *Dictionary of Modern Indian History, 1707–1947* (New Delhi, 1985), pp. 431–4; 62–6. For an excellent analytic account of the Maratha era, see Stewart Gordon, *The Marathas: 1600–1815* (Cambridge, 1993).

8.   Tod was put in charge of Mewar, Kotah, Bundi, Jaiselmer, and Sirohi. Tod's differences with David Ochterlony in Delhi and with other Company officials led in time to all these states, except Mewar, being withdrawn from his charge. When Jaiselmer was withdrawn in 1822 and he was dishonored by having his escort reduced, Tod resigned his post in Mewar in June and began his "travels in western India" prior to his departure for England from Bombay in February 1823.

9.   *Asiatic Researches*, the journal of the Asiatic Society, was founded in January 1784, by Sir William Jones four months after his arrival in Calcutta. The journal had the encouragement and support of India's first Governor-General, Warren Hastings (Robert Clive had preceded Hastings but as Governor-General of Bengal only). The first volume of *Asiatic Researches* was published in 1789. Four more volumes appeared over the ten years that William Jones served as President of Asiatic Society, each volume causing "a successively great sensation in Europe" (John Keay, *India Discovered: The Recovery of a Lost Civilization* [London: Harper Collins, 2001], p. 27). In his 1821 letters to Col. Colin MacKenzie Tod mentioned that he was not sending anything to the Asiatic Society "of which I am an unworthy

member; but dreading a critique it has lain quiet since the day written two years ago," and

> my enquiries are unabated, but I have not a single essay on any one subject. ... How or in what manner shall I attempt to reply to your letter? How enter the interminable field of Hindoo antiquity? Whither will it lead me? Where can I leave off? It is plunging me into a labyrinth of my own: but I have provided no clue for my exit and I may be left in the darkness of my own ideas without enlightening you. British Library, Add Mss 9868, F. 133, "Letter of Tod to MacKenzie, Oudipoor 17 February 1821", and Add Mss 9868, F. 114, as quoted in Freitag, "The Power which raised them from Ruin", p. 43.

Hastings was committed to Indian learning in part because he thought he should govern with the approbation (not the same as consent) of those he governed. He undertook measures to promote knowledge of the languages, texts and customs of the people of India starting with the languages of the text the scholar-administrators of the Asiatic Society were "discovering," Persian and Sanskrit, and extending to vernacular languages such as Bengali and Urdu. Hastings himself could speak Urdu and Bengali and commanded some Persian. Keay glosses the Hastings views this way:

> If British rule in India was to prosper and last, British administrators must themselves become partly Indianized. They must learn the languages, study the customs. The government must work within existing institutions, not try to impose a whole new set of Western ones. There must be intellectual exchange, not a walkover; and if there were flagrant abuses in Indian society they must be reformed from within, not proscribed from without (Keay, India Discovered, p. 23).

Tod follows the Hastings view of British rule in India, a view dia-metrically opposed to that advanced by James Mill and others. Mill's 1832 parliamentary testimony in anticipation of the Charter renewal in 1834 (to be characterized further below) articulates the alternative view while Tod's testimony builds on Warren Hastings' perspective.

10. O.P. Kejariwal, *The Asiatic Society of Bengal and the Discovery of India's Past* (New Delhi: Oxford University Press, 1988), p. xx.

11. Keay, *India Discovered*, p. 87.

12. Edward Said, *Orientalism* (New York: Pantheon Books, 1978). Said modifies his view and softens the structural determinism found in *Orientalism* in *Culture and Imperialism* (New York: Vintage Books, 1993).

13. Ronald Inden, *Imagining India* (Cambridge Mass.: Blackwell, 1990).

14. Such names as James Prinsep, Charles Wilkins, H.H. Wilson, H.T. Colebrooke. See Kejariwal, *The Asiatic Society* and Keay, *India Discovered*.

15. For a more nuanced, detailed, and annotated account of our critique of orientalism, see Lloyd I. Rudolph and Susanne Hoeber Rudolph, "Occidentalism and Orientalism: Perspectives on Legal Pluralism," in Sally C. Humphries (ed.), *Cultures of Scholarship* (Ann Arbor: University of Michigan Press, 1997), pp. 219–51.

16. Critical readings from the earliest reviews until today have dealt with factual "mistakes" with respect to lineages, dates, events, and with conceptual or theoretical "mistakes" such as, as in the case of Alfred Lyall, with too strongly discounting the clan or tribal aspect of Rajput society and rule in order to privilege the feudal aspect. With the recent exception of Norbert Peabody's 1996 critique of Ronald Inden's reading in *Imagining India* (Oxford, 1990), they have

not dealt with tropes and analogies that shaped his conceptual imagination and narratives (N. Peabody, "Tod's *Rajasthan* and the Boundaries of Imperial Rule in Nineteenth-century India," *Modern Asian Studies*, 30, 1 [1996]).

17. Tod draws upon Henry Hallam's *View of the State of Europe during the Middle Ages*, 2 vols (London, 1818). The only comprehensive intellectual-cum-biographical study of Hallam known to us is Peter Clark's *Henry Hallam* (Boston: Twayne Publishers, 1982). Clark provides detailed bibliographical references to works by and about Hallam. He reports *inter alia* that during Hallam's lifetime there were 11 editions of the *Middle Ages*. After Hallams' death in 1859 two more editions of the *Middle Ages* were published in 1868 and 1872. In the United States the *Middle Ages* was even more successful: four editions were published there in the 1880s and 1890s. In France, Hallam's work went through four editions and in Italy one. Clark tells us that "In his day (Hallam) was regarded as the doyen of English historians. ... The framework he used and the conclusions he reached were substantially those of his successors ... Stubbs, Froude and Gardiner ... because the Victorian historians were working with the same terms of reference. Hallam saw himself as a philosophical historian—in the tradition of Hume, Robertson, and Gibbon. Thus Hallam is an essential link between Hume and Stubbs. ... His work had an appeal to the generation of 1830–70, and helped in the making of the historical consciousness of that generation. ... The Queen, Gladstone, and Disraeli all read (his works)." Apart from Clark's work, for Hallam's life, including the Hallam family's relationship to Alfred Tennyson, see A.S. Byatt's fictionalized account in *Angels and Insects* (London: Chatto & Windus Ltd., 1992). *In Memoriam* (1850), the work that established Tennyson's reputation, was written to

remember Arthur Hallam, Henry's son, the fiancé of Tennyson's sister, whose youthful death struck an important chord in Romantic consciousness. As we point out later, Tod celebrated youthful, heroic death. A searching critique of Tod's conception of feudalism can be found in Chapter 1, "Something Very Like Feudalism," in Robert Stern's *The Cat and the Lion: Jaipur State in the British Raj* (Leiden: Brill Academic Publishing, 1988).

18. For insightful and telling interpretations *inter alia* of Montesquieu, Millar, and Hume, see Albert O. Hirschman, *The Passions and the Interests: Political Arguments for Capitalism before Its Triumph* (Princeton: Princeton University Press, 1997). For Gibbon see the introduction by David Womersley in his recently edited republication of Edward Gibbon, *The History of the Rise and Fall of the Roman Empire* (London, 1994), Vol. I, pp. xi–cviii. Tod cites Gibbon's *Miscellaneous Work*, Vol. III.

19. These passages are from Lieut.-Col. James Tod, *The Annals and Antiquities of Rajasthan or, The Central and Western Rajpoot States of India*, two volumes in one with a preface by Douglas Sladen (London, 1914; reprinted in 1923 and 1950), Vol. I, pp. 107–8.

20. The quote from *Childe Harold* is from Canto iii and is cited in the *Annals*, Vol. 1, p. 612. Tod cites Byron again in Vol. 2 (p. 510) when deploring the Company's policy toward cultivation of opium, "this execrable and demoralising plant." "We have saved Rajpootana," he writes, "from political ruin; but the boon of mere existence will be valueless if we fail to restore the moral energies of her population; for of this fine region and noble race we might say, as Byron does of Greece—'Tis Greece—but living Greece no more!'."

21. Martin Bernal, *Black Athena* (New Brunswick NJ: Rutgers University Press, 1990), Vol. 1, p. 291.

22. Herman, *How the Scots*, p. 226. Herman says of Gibbon "although English (he) modeled his work closely on the Scottish and Edinburgh historical school. ... One of his closest friends was Adam Ferguson, but his other heroes were Hume and Smith, whose new book, *The Wealth of Nations*," Gibbon called "the most profound and systematic treatise on the great objects of trade and revenue which had ever been published in any age or century." When Hume wrote to Gibbon praising his new history, Gibbon said the letter "repaid the labour of ten years" (pp. 225-6).

23. These are the persons associated with the Scottish enlightenment that Tod cites in "Sketch of the Feudal System in Rajasthan" (Vol. I, pp. 107-58). As has been noted above, he relies in this section most heavily on Henry Hallam but Montesquieu is also of considerable importance for Tod's formulation.

24. Herman, *How the Scots*, pp. 308-10. For much of the detail and some of the interpretation of Scottish Romanticism We are indebted to Herman's chapter on Scott—"The Last Minstrel: Sir Walter Scott and the Highland Revival" (pp. 291-319). Herman argues that Scott's novels introduced several key components of "modern consciousness" including cultural conflict. History is presented as a series of "culture wars": Frank versus Saracen (in *The Talisman*), Jew versus Christian (in *Ivanhoe*), Norman versus Saxon, Scotsman versus Englishman, Lowlander versus Highlander, Presbyterian versus Episcopalian. ... Which side is superior, and which deserves to lose, is never fully resolved." (p. 310).

25. Herman, *How the Scots*, p. 310.

26. For example, Edmund Burke, Shelley, Wordsworth, Coleridge, Keats, Sir Walter Scott, Lord Byron; Edward Gibbon.

27.   See Nigel Leask, *British Romantic Writers and the East: Anxieties of Empire* (Cambridge: Routledge, 1993).

28.   Leask, *British Romantic Writers*, p. 13.

29.   Saloombra, estate of the Chandawat leader. He led Mewar forces in the battle. It is common to call particular persons by the name of their estate.

30.   Tod, *Annals* (ed. Douglas Sladen, 1920, 2 vols in 1), Vol. 1, p. 201.

31.   Sinha and Das Gupta (eds.), *Ochterlony Papers (1818–1825)*. About one-third of 230 Rajputana Residency Records printed in this volume present the voice and views of Tod or Ochterlony. Like the parliamentary clash between James Mill and James Tod, these documents reveal profound ideological and policy differences between the two men involved.

32.   James Mill, "Testimony to Parliament dated 16 February, 1832, Reports from Committees, Session 6. December 1831–16 August 1832," in *Minutes of Evidence Taken before the Select Committee on the Affairs of the East India Company, VI: Political or Foreign, Vols VII, XIV* (London: House of Commons, Parliament of England, 1832), pp. 3–10; and James Tod. "Testimony to Parliament, Reports from Committees, Session 6 December 1831–16 August 1832, Appendix 13." *Minutes of Evidence Taken before the Select Committee on the Affairs of the East India Company, VI: Political or Foreign, Vols VII XIV* (London: House of Commons, Parliament of England, 1832), pp. 122–35, both reprinted in Part II of this volume.

33.   Uday Singh Mehta, *Liberalism and Empire: A Study in Nineteenth Liberal Thought* (Chicago, 1999). Mehta contrasts Burke's commitment to the naturalness of difference with Locke's commitment to

the naturalness of uniformity. Burke, he tells us, "reflected with great seriousness on the situation in which the exercise of power and authority was implicated with considerations of cultural and racial diversity, contrasting civilizational unities, the absence of ... consensual government, and alternative forms of political identity and legitimacy" (pp. 134–55). If difference was all for Burke, if persons were always and inevitably marked, for the liberal Locke, sameness was all. Human nature was the same everywhere and always. Locke articulates "liberal universalism" from which "... claims can be made because they derive from certain characteristics that are common to all human being" (pp. 51–2).

34. Michael Herzfeld opens his *Anthropology through the Looking Glass: Critical Ethnography in the Margins of Europe* (Cambridge: Cambridge University Press, 1987; 1989) with the following sentence: "Ancient Greece is the idealized spiritual and intellectual ancestor of Europe" (p. 1). For views of this large and contested interpretation see his *Ours Once and More: Folklore, Ideology, and the Making of Modern Greece* (Texas: University of Texas Press, 1982), in particular Chapter 1, "Past Glories, Present Politics" (pp. 3–23), as well as Chapter 1, "Romanticism and Hellenism: Burdens of Otherness" in his *Anthropology through the Looking Glass* (pp. 1–27). More than any other person, Adamantios Koraes (1748–1833) invented the imagined community of Hellenic Greeks. *Inter alia* he aroused Jefferson's interest in the cause of Greek liberty.

35. Leask, *British Romantic Writers*.

36. Preface to Percy B. Shelly, *Hellas* (1821).

37. Peabody refers to "The Rajput Nation" and discusses "The nation in early nineteenth-century thought" and "Imperialism,

nationalism, and the social construction of difference." According to Peabody "... Tod's notion of the nation was based on differentiation of insider from outsider, or native from foreigner, categories whose context dependency makes them classic examples of 'group shifters'" (Peabody, "Tod's *Rajasthan*", pp. 204–11; the reference to Bentinck is at p. 209).

38. An extensive and detailed account of Buckingham's conflict with the East India Company, particularly with the acting Governor-General John Adam, was published in January 1824, in the first volume and number of *The Oriental Herald* under the title "Appeal of a Governor-General to Public Opinion in India" which is, in fact, Buckingham's 71-page answer to John Adam's "Statement of Facts connected with the Removal from India of Mr. Buckingham, Late Editor of the *Calcutta Journal*" (pp. 6–77). The ideological and policy battle between Tod and Ochterlony can be followed in detail in Sinha and Das Gupta, *Selections from Ochterlony Papers*.

39. The social ideology of *varna* appears in the *Rig Veda*, *The Laws of Manu*, and other brahmanical texts and was accepted until recently as authoritative by "Indologists" from Max Müller to Max Weber to Louis Dumont. *Varna* social ideology depicted "caste" in terms of brahmans (priests), kshatriyas (warrior rulers), vaishyas (merchants), shudras (manual workers, including peasants and artisans), and untouchables (*mlecchas* or "foreigners"; conquered people or Dasas; those outside the caste system including latter day "unclean" or "impure" "untouchables" whom the British, and after independence, the Government of India, designated "scheduled castes"). The origin myth from the *Rig Veda* speaks of the "Sacrifice of the Cosmic Man"; brahmans issued from his mouth, kshatriyas from his arms; vaishyas

from his thighs and shudras from his feet. Brahmans, kshatriyas, and vaishyas were "twice born," that is, taught sacred knowledge, they donned a sacred thread at puberty signifying their spiritual rebirth. Recent scholarship has denaturalized *varna* and caste, depicting them as historically constructed and subject to continuous change. See, for example, Romila Thapar, *Ancient Indian Social History: Some Interpretations* (New Delhi: Orient Longmans, 1978); our *Modernity of Tradition* (Chicago: University of Chicago Press, 1967); and Nicholas Dirks, *The Hollow Crown: Ethnohistory of an Indian Kingdom* (Cambridge: Cambridge University Press, 1987).

40.   For an elaboration of British views of caste in the context of its transformations, see our *Modernity of Tradition*, pp. 15-154.

41.   See Florence S. Boos (ed.), *History and Communalism: Essay in Victorian Medievalism* (New York: Garland Publishing, 1992). Boos herself writes that the attraction of medievalism arose from "a sense of the 'medieval' as *alternative culture* ... alternative both to contemporary capitalist and imperialist *realpolitics*, and to the unrealities of their conventional classical education ..." (p. 13). For Tod, writing well before the turn of the century, the classical had yet to lose its charm.

42.   For an account of Victoria's keenness about being made Empress of India see Stanley Weintraub, *Victoria: An Intimate Biography* (New York: Dutton, 1987), pp. 413-20. The Queen, Weintraub writes, "was anxious about her dignity." The unification of Germany under Prussia had made her daughter, Vicky, a future empress. When crowned, Vicky might, in the absence of Parliamentary action, have precedence over her. Disraeli responded to the Queen's request by shepherding an official titles bill through Parliament (pp. 413-14).

43. For the historical circumstances and moral and psychological grounding of British racial ideology about martial and non-martial races, see our *The Modernity of Tradition*, pp. 165–7:

> Within twenty years of the deliberate exclusion of United Province brahmans from the Bengal Army because of their leading role in the rebellion of 1857, the idea that brahmans lacked fighting qualities had become prevailing opinion ... in English minds at the end of the century, the distinction (between martial and non-martial) was stressed as much for its instrumental utility in the imperialist theory as for its academic interest as a description of caste or regional character. The "martial" races for the most part adhered to the British raj, not because they were martial ... but for political considerations, the Rajputs because they were the princes of states whose autonomy was threatened by a self-governing India, the Muslims because they feared a Hindu majority in independent India ... Those described as the non-martial races produced nationalism.

44. See Chapter XIV, "The Martial Classes" of Philip Mason, *A Matter of Honour: An Account of the Indian Army, Its Officers and Men* (London: J. Cape, 1986), pp. 341–61, particularly "2: Lord Roberts and His Views," pp. 345–50.

45. MacMunn averred: "The mass of the people of India have neither martial aptitude nor physical courage." Of India's 350 million people only 35 million qualified as martial races and of these only 3 million were males between 20 and 35 years of age. Mason adds that "the idea that some people will make soldiers and some will not is of course much older than the British. It is implicit in the Hindu caste system; no raja would have the money-lender or the trader castes to bear arms. But it was the British, after the Mutiny, step by step, who formulated and codified the principle, turning what

had been a matter of practical choice into a dogma proclaimed with theological rigour." (Mason, *Honour*, pp. 348-9).

46. For Jones' view see Thomas R. Trautman, *Aryans and British India* (New Delhi: Yoda Press, 2004), Chapter 2, "The Mosaic Ethnology of Asiatick Jones," pp. 28-61.

47. Although Tod—and others—in the 1820s already spoke of a potential Russian threat to India, it was Rudyard Kipling's *Kim* that introduced the English-speaking world to the metaphor of the "Great Game" in Asia. Tod argued for a British–Rajput alliance in part to have the strength on the subcontinent to face Russian ambitions. For the state of play after the time of the Soviet invasion of Afghanistan, see Lloyd I. Rudolph, "The Great Game in Asia: Revisited and Revised," *Crossroads: An International Socio-Political Journal*, 16 (1985). For an overview see Peter Hopkirk, *The Great Game: On Secret Service in High Asia* (London: Murray, 1992).

48. Rajput history and images influenced the thinking and writing of eminent Bengalis including Henry Louis DeRozio, Bankim Chandra Chatterji, and Rabindranath Tagore (see his *Kathu-o-Kahini* for several Rajput poems, including one expressing his disillusionment after actually visiting Rajasthan in the late 1930s). Our thanks to the late Sujit Mukherjee for calling this poem to our attention and doing a rough translation for us. General works on the influence of Rajput history and legend on nationalist consciousness, starting with consciousness in Bengal, include Papia Chakrabarty, *Hindu Response to Nationalist Ferment: Bengal 1909–1935* (Calcutta: Subarnarekha, 1992); Amrita Lal De, *The Student's History of Rajpootana, Being an Account of the Princes of Rajpootana from the Earliest Ages to the Modern Times* (Calcutta, 1889); Dalia Ray, *The Bengal Revolutionaries and Freedom Movement* (New Delhi: Cosmo Publications, 1990); Ashis

Sanyal, *Contributions of Bengali Writers to National Freedom Movement* (Calcutta: Model Publishing, 1989). We are indebted to Jason Freitag's "The Power Which Raised Them from Ruin" for some of these references.

49. Gandhi, *Collected Works*, 48, p. 307.

50. Discourse about "primitive" is insightfully explored in Marianna Torgovnick's *Gone Primitive: Savage Intellects, Modern Lives* (Chicago: University of Chicago Press, 1990). Torgovnick tells us that "... primitive societies or the general idea of the primitive becomes a place to project our feelings about the present and to draw blueprints of the future. Sometimes narratives about primitive societies become allegories of modernization that resist seeing themselves or presenting themselves as allegories" (p. 244).

51. The quotation is from the historical introduction to *Rajputana and Ajmer: List of Ruling Princes, Chiefs and Leading Personages* (Calcutta: Government of India, 1931). This is the sixth edition of a "work projected in 1890 by Colonel G.H. Trevor, C.S.I., Agent to the Governor-General for Rajputana ... and put together by C.S. Bayley, C.S., then Political Agent, Bikaner." Some of the account in the historical introduction was written as early as 1879.

52. Sir Walter Lawrence, *The India We Served* (London: Cassel and Company Ltd., 1928), p. 56. Here we see how "Rajput" took on gentlemanly overtones. For narratives, histories, and tropes of "gentleman," see Rupert Wilkinson, *Gentlemanly Power* (New York: Oxford University Press, 1964).

53. Norman Ziegler's study of the *Khyāt* of Nainsi, a seventeenth-century Jodhpur administrator, shows how Mughal administrative categories and practices were assimilated into Rajput political ideas and practices. It also suggests the creation of a more complex and

hierarchical status order on analogies with Mughal court society. Ziegler's study of fifteenth-century Rajput folksongs and tales is striking for the absence in them of the florid literary and cultural embellishments of the later bardic accounts, and suggests that Kolff's characterizations of Rajputs, of which more below, as plain fighting men of diverse origins may apply to Rajputs in Rajputana as well as in other parts of North India ("The Seventeenth Century Chronicles of Marvara: A Study in the Evolution and Use of Oral Traditions in Western India," *History in Africa*, 3 (1976); "Marvari Historical Chronicles: Sources for the Social and Cultural History of Rajasthan," *Indian Economic and Social History Review*, 13 [1976]). Nicholas Dirks, in his *The Hollow Crown*, argues that the political processes associated with kingship rather than canonical texts or brahmanic understandings determined social preference and standing, including caste identity and privileges. South Indian kings, he argues, used symbolic and material resources under their control to reshape or constitute status orders and castes.

54.   During the sixteenth and seventeenth centuries, the top layer of Rajputs (in Rajputana), encouraged by the openings presented by the Mughal state and helped by the expertise of their bards, tended to ... articulate new norms of Rajput behavior. Bards had always encouraged their Rajput employers to assume aristocratic self-images closely linked with myths of origin that established their status as kshatriyas and traced back their genealogies to, for instance, the great dynasties of ancient Indian history. ... The tendency to interpret Rajput history in genealogical terms was later inherited by Tod and other British administrators ... something like a new Rajput Great Tradition emerged (in the

seventeenth and eighteenth centuries) which could recognize little else than unilineal kin bodies as the elements of which genuine Rajput history ought to be made up. Dirk H.A. Kolff, *Naukar, Rajput and Sepoy: The Ethnohistory of the Military Labour Market in Hindustan, 1450–1850* (Cambridge: Cambridge University Press, 1990), pp. 72–3.

Kolff sees the "original Rajputs" as an open status group in which, as late as the nineteenth century, included "errant soldier, migrant labourer, or pack-animal trader." This interpretation is not accepted by many contemporary Rajputs who hold that Rajputs are descended from an historical Ram or from his sons. For a debate about Rajput status a generation ago, see Rushton Coulborn (ed.), *Feudalism in History* (Princeton NJ: Princeton University Press, 1956) and the debate that followed about "feudalism" as a universal category. For example, did it exist as a "stage" of development in India and Japan? The debate at that time about whether Rajputs in India were a feudal status category or class was innocent of the understanding suggested here that Tod, who established the term for India, used Henry Hallam's reading of medieval feudalism as the core of his historiographical construction of feudalism in India.

55. Aspects of these perceptions and attitudes can be gleaned from E.M. Forster's *Passage to India* and Paul Scott's four-volume *The Jewel in the Crown*. Philip Woodruff's *The Men Who Ruled India*, 2 vols (London: Jonathan Cape, 1953–4) traces the evolution of East India Company and Indian Civil Service (ICS) mentalities. Clive Dewey's recent study shows the complexity of cultural provenance, motive, and intention among several prominent late nineteenth-century ICS officers (C. Dewey, *Anglo-Indian Attitudes: The*

Mind of the Indian Civil Servant [London and Rio Grande: The Hambledon Press, 1993]).

56. In the opening decades of the nineteenth century, the Company ended lingering Maratha pretensions to imperial status, defeated and pacified the Pindaris, and gradually closed the peasant-based military labor market by confining military recruitment to high caste Hindus. As a result, according to Dirk Kolff, "The Company largely achieved the demilitarisation ... of politics at the regional level." By 1850, "British North India was almost totally demilitarised ..." (Kolff, *Naukar, Rajput and Sepoy*, p. 188). After the bloody and almost successful revolt in 1857 by alienated sepoys, talukdars, and princes, a Government of India Act had replaced East India Company with Crown rule. A viceroy representing the British Queen now stood in the place of the Mughal Emperor as the hegemonic power on the Indian subcontinent. In time, the treaties became an important source for the doctrine of paramountcy. See S.N. Sen, *Eighteen Fifty-Seven* (New Delhi: Government of India, 1957) and Ainslee T. Embree (ed.), *India in 1857: The Revolt Against Foreign Rule* (New York: D.C. Heath, 1963).

57. See Introduction, Part 1. "Provenance: Making a Self at the Jodhpur Court," in Susanne Hoeber Rudolph and Lloyd I. Rudolph (with Mohan Singh Kanota), *Reversing the Gaze; Amar Singh's Diary, A Colonial Subject's Narrative of Imperial India* (New Delhi: Oxford University Press, 2000), pp. 1–15.

58. See our essay, "Rajputana Under British Paramountcy: The Failure of Indirect Rule," in Lloyd I. Rudolph and Susanne Hoeber Rudolph, *Essays on Rajputana* (New Delhi: Concept Publishing, 1984), pp. 3–37. See also Part VI, "Princely Courts in Imperial Space,"

of our *Reversing the Gaze*, pp. 467–556. For the "integration" of the princely states see *inter alia* V.P. Menon, *Story of the Integration of the Princely States* (New Delhi: Orient Longmans, 1955) and *The Transfer of Power* (New Delhi: Orient Longmans, 1957).

59. See our essay, "The Political Modernization of an Indian Feudal Order: An Analysis of Rajput Adaptation in Rajasthan" in Lloyd I. Rudolph and Susanne Hoeber Rudolph, *Essays on Rajputana*, pp. 38–78.

60. For a discussion on authenticity in the context of identity and replication, see our 2002 Ryerson Lecture at the University of Chicago, "Engaging Subjective Knowledge: Narratives of and by the Self in the Amar Singh Diary," *The University of Chicago Record*, 36, 4 (2002).

2 Tod vs Mill*

Clashing Perspectives on British Rule in India and Indian Civilization: An Analysis Based on James Tod's and James Mill's 1832 Parliamentary Testimony

In 1832 James Tod and James Mill gave testimony to a Parliamentary committee assessing the performance of the East India Company in India.[1] The Committee's job was to make recommendations for East India Company Charter revision the following year. Their testimony frames radically contrasting views not only of Company rule and the value of India's civilization but also of the nature of inquiry and knowledge. They read the past differently and foresee a different future.

Tod speaks from the Romantic Orientalist perspective of William Jones and the Asiatic Society of Bengal, Mill from the Utilitarian perspective of Jeremy Bentham's philosophical radicalism. The Company's adoption of a world view and policies based on Mill's Utilitarian rationalism leads to the destruction of Company rule in the rebellion of 1857. Tod's Orientalist romanticism regains primacy in the world view and policies of Queen Victoria's 1858 Proclamation replacing Company with Crown rule. The contestation between an "orientalist" perspective that recognizes difference and respects Indian civilization[2] and Indians' potential for self-rule and a "Utilitarian" perspective that denies difference yet views India as a barbarian country incapable of self-rule continued to animate British thought and policy for the hundred years between Victoria's 1858 Proclamation and Indian independence in 1947.[3]

What light do the lives and experience of the two men who testified before Parliament in 1832 about the past, present, and future of the East India Company rule in India throw on their testimony? James Mill was James Tod's senior by nine years; Mill was born in 1773, Tod in 1782. Both were Scottish. Mill was born there, the son of "a mild-mannered and devout shoemaker" and a socially ambitious mother,[4] Tod was born in Islington, then a London suburb, the son of a father whose family was said to be ancient and honored,[5] and an American born mother, Mary Heatly. Both of her brothers, James Tod's uncles, served in the Bengal Civil Service. She is described as "a lady remarkable for her intellectual accomplishments and for the vigour of her understanding."[6]

After trying unsuccessfully for eight years to be teacher and a preacher, Mill left Scotland for London in 1802 to try a career in journalism at which he was moderately successful. The two great successes of his life were his relationship as a friend and colleague with the philosophical radical, Jeremy Bentham, whom he met in 1808, and his authorship and publication in 1818 of the three-volume *History of British India*. It took 12 years to research and write but it made him famous and garnered an appointment in 1819 at the East India Company as an Assistant Examiner. By 1830, six years before his death, he was appointed Head Examiner at the East India Company.

Mill wrote his enormously influential[7] indictment of India, the *History of British India*, without visiting India or knowing an Indian language. Tod arrived in Calcutta in 1799 as a 17-year-old cadet assigned to the Second European regiment. His varied 24 years included some remarkable tasks and feats. He did for Central and Western India, the India that stretched from Saurashtra in the far west to the Doab in Central India, what Lewis and Clark at about the same time were doing for the Louisiana Purchase, exploring, surveying, and mapping unknown territory. Like them, he lived and suffered "under canvas" in remote areas and in isolated circumstances for years on end. He created an intelligence service that in 1817 made possible the Company's victory in the third Anglo-Maratha war, a victory that established Company hegemony on the Indian subcontinent. Most important in four short years, 1818 to 1822, as the Company's Political Agent in Mewar [today's Udaipur] he gathered the documents and acquired the learning that helped to write a monumental empathetic work about the other, *The Annals and Antiquities of Rajasthan*. Mill's life and learning led him to mock and despise the other, Tod's life and learning led him to respect, even to identify with, the other. Their parliamentary testimony in 1832 about Company rule and India's civilization reflected these differences.

Before examining Tod's "Orientalist" and Mill's "Utilitarian" testimony in 1832, we want to locate what they had to say within the Company's "*longue duree*,"[8] the century between the battle of Plassey in 1757 and Queen Victoria's Proclamation in 1858. Plassey opened the era of Company raj; Queen Victoria's Proclamation ended it. Clive's victory at Plassey gave the Company a foothold on sovereignty in India, a foothold that the first Governor General, Warren Hastings [1774–85], and his successors vastly expanded. The Company's victory over Tipu Sultan in 1799 and its final victory over the Marathas in 1817 made the Company the hegemonic power on the subcontinent and the de facto successor to the moribund Mughal Empire in India.

During the *longue duree* of Company *raj* we witness the effect of a changing equation between power and culture. The less British power, the more the British recognize and respect Indian culture, the more British power, the less the British recognize and respect Indian culture.[9] In the early years, when British power in the form of the East India Company's presence on the Indian sub-continent is limited and contingent, when the Company's presence depends on the permission of the Moghul emperor and continues on his sufferance, the Orientalists of the Asiatic Society of Bengal "discover" and celebrate India's languages and civilizations. James Tod can be counted as an Orientalist.[10] His two-volume major work, *The Annals and Antiquities of Rajasthan* [1829 and 1832], celebrates Rajput history, society, and culture. James Mill can be counted as a Utilitarian and a fellow traveling Evangelical.[11] His immensely influential[12] three-volume work, *History of British India* [1817], excoriates India's culture and rulers.

With benefit of hindsight, we can see that as the Company's power expands the orientalists are challenged, then displaced by Utilitarians and Evangelicals. A critical turning point came in 1835. The newly appointed law member in the Utilitarian administration of Governor General Lord William Bentinck, Thomas Babington Macauley, convinced a majority of Bentinck's Council to adopt his Minute on Education. Doing so reversed a half century of support for an Orientalist policy of supporting Indian learning and languages and replaced it with a policy that gave primacy to education in English about western knowledge. As Macauley famously put it at the time: "... all the books written in the Sanskrit language [are] ... less valuable than what may be found in ... abridgements used at preparatory schools in England." Macauley's goal was to form "a class of persons, Indian in blood and colour, but English in taste, in opinions, in morals, and in intellect."[13] The voices, views and policies of Utilitarians such as William Bentinck and Thomas Macauley, and Evangelicals such as Charles Grant and Alexander Duff displace those of Orientalists such as Warren Hastings, Sir William Jones, Henry Thomas Colebrooke, and Henry Hayman Wilson. The value of Tod's and Mill's 1832 parliamentary testimony lies in the stark confrontation it offers 75 years after Plassey and 25 years before Queen Victoria's proclamation between an orientalist and a Utilitarian perspective on Indian civilization and rule.

We have referred to Mill as a fellow traveling Evangelical. It is not often appreciated that he spent four years studying for the ministry [1794–98], was licensed to preach in 1798 and, after failing to secure a position, spent four more frustrating and difficult years as an itinerant preacher. If, after meeting and joining forces with Jeremy Bentham in 1808, he became a Utilitarian and a rationalist, he did not stop being an evangelical Christian. The abhorrence for Hindu religion found in his *History of British India*, particularly in chapter 10 of Book II, arose as much from an Evangelical Christian as from Utilitarian world view. If Bentinck was the principal agent of Utilitarianism in India,[14] Mill's fellow Scot, Alexander Duff, was the principal agent of Evangelical Christianity.[15] Like Macauley who used English-medium education to promote western learning in India, Duff used English-medium education to introduce Christianity to successive generations of young Indians. Duff went beyond Macauley's view that Indian knowledge was worthless. Like Mill he found Indian culture as expressed in Hindu religion depraved: "of all the systems of false religion ever fabricated by the perverse ingenuity of fallen men, Hinduism is surely the most stupendous."[16]

In 1857 the rebellion by poorly paid, harshly disciplined and dishonored[17] *sepoys* [soldiers] of the Company's Bengal Army and by rulers whose kingdoms had been conquered or "annexed"[18] unexpectedly and suddenly reversed the power equation. British forces were defeated; British officers and men and British civilians were killed; Indian forces captured and occupied Delhi where the Mughal Emperor, Bahadur Shah II, was released from confinement and restored to his throne. Luckily for the restoration of British rule, the conclusion of the Crimean War made it possible to bring British soldiers by sea to re-enforce the defeated and demoralized British garrison in India. Also fortunate for the British cause was the willingness of Sikh troops from the recently conquered Punjab to fight on behalf of the restoration of British rule. Contributing to turning the tide was the de-centered nature of the rebellion and its lack of ideological coherence and effective leadership.[19]

What began in May 1857 was more or less over by April 1858. But the shock of rebellion and defeat was both immediate and enduring. Overnight, British power in India had collapsed. In the wake of that collapse, Indian culture and governance were restored. The Orientalist world view of William Jones and

James Tod displaced the Utilitarian and Evangelical world view of William Bentinck and Alexander Duff. Mill's policy of eradicating Indian civilization and replacing Indian rule was replaced by Tod's of respecting Indian civilization and recognizing Indian rule.

In August 1858, Queen Victoria issued a Proclamation that replaced East India Company rule with Crown rule, assured India's rulers that their sovereignty was secure[20] and called upon them to be "loyal feudatories of the Crown." More important, the Queen declared "it to be our royal will and pleasure that none be in anywise favoured, none molested or disquieted, by reason of their religious faith or observances, but that all shall alike enjoy the equal and impartial protection of the law; and we do strictly charge and enjoin all those who may be in authority under us that they abstain from all interference with religious belief or worship of any of our subjects on pain of our highest displeasure."[21]

In 1857 British power in India had been temporarily shattered. The 1858 Proclamation reversed course. It replaced Company rule with Crown rule. Instead of conquering or "annexing" India's kingdoms and erasing and displacing India's civilization and languages in the name of Utilitarianism and Evangelicalism, as governor generals from Bentinck to Dalhousie had done, the Proclamation followed Tod's advice by recognizing the suzerainty of India's rulers, welcoming them as "loyal feudatories" of the Crown, and promising to respect and honor India's religions and civilization.

When James Tod and James Mill testified before a Parliamentary committee in 1832 in anticipation of charter reform, the Company had "ruled" in India for 75 years. They and the Parliamentary committee didn't know that within 25 years Company raj would end.[22]

At the broadest level of policy, Tod's "Orientalist" world view led him to affirm the virtues and expediency of indirect rule, i.e. recognizing the suzerainty of the right kind of Indian rulers.[23] Mill's "Utilitarian" world view led him to argue for the efficiency and efficacy of direct rule, i.e. deposing India's rulers and putting British administrators in the Company's service in charge of governing the Indian subcontinent.[24]

Tod prefaced his written answers to the Parliamentary Committee's questions by assuring its members that his opinions "... are given without regard to any consideration but the duty which, at this crisis, requires every Indian functionary to speak without reserve. If any influence preponderates, it is, perhaps, in favour of the governed; and with this object in view, if I should utter truths somewhat unpalatable, I disclaim every motive but the desire of being instrumental to good."[25]

Mill's attitude toward "the governed" was that they should be subdued and cowed.[26] Their role was to be passive and obedient. He told the Committee: "The simple mode of considering our position in India is to consider the extent actually pervaded by our power, really and truly under our dominion; ...." The power of the subsidiary and protected princes is "entirely nominal." With respect to all of them, we take the military powers of government entirely into our own hands. Now if it is considered what the military power implies; that it is, in truth, *the whole power*, [emphasis added] it will be seen that what we do with those protected princes is merely to delegate to them the powers of internal administration, which, in such a case in their hands, are in truth the powers of oppressing their subjects. This unfortunate intermediate state between British government and native, is filled up with nothing but abomination.

If Mill urged the Parliament to rid the Company of the "abomination" of indirect rule, Tod urged it to preserve and improve it:

Unless it be intended to introduce, contrary to the faith of our treaties, our *direct* [Tod's emphasis] rule into these states, the first and most important point is to fix the rate of tribute, and to fix it as low as possible; since the sacrifice of a lac [100,000] or two, while it will be a trifle to us, will be a vast benefit to these impoverished princes, whose good-will will be proportioned to the comfort and respectability we ensure to them.

"In all those states," he continued, "there exist the materials of government; and the cement that has held them together for a period of from 700 to 1,000 years is still undestroyed ..."

Tod's and Mill's radically opposed views about the defence of the subcontinent provided another context for them to clash over indirect and direct rule. When asked by a Committee member if the defence "of our dominions was more easy from having the whole of India, not a part merely?" Mill replied that it was greatly preferable to control the whole: "It is not easy," he told the committee, "to find a great empire with so small a frontier to defend as India, when you possess the whole; as in three parts it is bounded by the sea, and in the other by mountains, which can only be passed at a few places, or through a desert scarcely passable at all ..."

Tod thought about the internal and external security of India in very different terms. It was best maintained by the rulers of India's kingdoms. "If the *spirit* of the treaties be upheld," [27] he argued, "it is no exaggeration to say, that, with a few years of prosperity, we could oppose to any enemy [such as the Russians][28] upon this one only vulnerable frontier [in the Northwest], at least 50,000 Rajpoots, headed by their respective princes, who would die in our defence."[29]

Mill as we have seen considers indirect rule, what is referred to in 1832 as "the subsidiary system," an "abomination." Indirect rule is the worst of all because under it British power protects Indian rulers against the revolts their oppression would generate. Mill explains that "It has been found by experience that misgovernment under ... divided rule [goes] ... to its utmost extent, far beyond its ordinary limits ... in India ... The causes are found in the absence of a check on a prince's power. In the ordinary state of things in India ... the princes stood in awe of their subjects." Mill alleges that insurrection against oppression was the general practice of the country. The princes knew that when mismanagement and oppression went to a certain extent, there would be revolt, and that they would stand a chance of being tumbled from their throne, and a successful leader of the insurgents put in their place. This check is, by our interference, totally taken away. ... The people know that any attempt of theirs would be utterly unavailing against our irresistible power. Accordingly no such thought occurs to them, and they submit to every degree of oppression that befalls them.

Ironically, the 1857 rebellion confirmed Mill's view that "insurrection against oppression was the general practice of the country."

Tod agrees with Mill that India's rulers have become oppressive but Tod's cure is radically different from Mill's, conquest and direct rule. In echoes of Edmund Burke's concept of the "ancient constitution" and of Montesquieu's concept of "intermediary powers," Tod tells the Parliamentary committee that "We have completely destroyed the ancient balance of power, which often ended in the deposal or death of a tyrant."[30] He explains that one of the effects of our alliances with the states of Rajpootana has been "the abolition of all those wholesome checks which restrained the passions of their princes."

Indirect rule would have succeeded—and can succeed—if Company interventions in support of rulers had not helped—and do not help—Indian rulers to crush the feudal aristocracies

that held them in check. These misplaced interventions happened as a result of "applying our own monarchical principles.
... we recognise only the immediate power with whom we
treated, and whom we engage to support against all enemies,
internal and external." The ruler finds that he is "free from the
fear of a re-action amongst his feudatory kinsmen ... no neighbour prince dare give sanctuary to his victims." If "insatiate
avarice" leads him "to visit the merchant and cultivator with
contributions or exorbitant taxes on their labour, the sufferers
are no longer able to emigrate to neighboring kingdoms." "Our
alliance," he concludes, has had the effect of "having completely neutralized all the checks that avarice or tyranny had to
fear from the hatred of their chiefs or subjects."[31]

For Mill the feudal aristocracy to whom Tod looked to
check tyranny and protect liberty was part and parcel of the
"abomination" known as the subsidiary system. Mill, an up-
from-the-bootstraps Scot, had an "abiding hatred" for the privileges and advantages of an aristocracy, the very intermediary
powers that Montesquieu and Tod held blocked tyranny and
protected liberty.[32]

Mill assured the committee that direct rule by British
administrators was the only way to govern India. What the
ordinary man, the peasant cultivator, wanted, was order and
efficiency. "In my opinion," he told the Parliamentary
Committee, "the best thing for the happiness of the people is,
that our government should be nominally, as well as really,
extended over those territories ... [and] that our own modes of

governing should be adopted, and our own people put in the charge of the government."

Unlike Tod, who, as we have seen, testified that "in all those states [of Rajpootana] there exist the materials of government; and the cement that has held them together for a period of from 700 to 1,000 years ...,"[33] for Mill legitimacy and identity didn't matter in the un-marked world of reason. "The mass of the people," he argued, "care very little by what sort of persons they are governed. They hardly think at all about the matter. ... if they find themselves at peace in their dwellings and their fields, and are not burthened [sic] by heavy annual exactions, they are equally contented whether their comfort is under rulers with turbans or hats." Mill would agree with Alexander Pope:

> For forms of government let fools contest;
> Whate'er is best administer'd is best:[34]

The connection to ancient lineage, valorous deeds, and the mystique of royal ritual that Tod celebrated Mill found absurd and irrational. "Nothing is more ridiculous," Mill told the Parliamentary committee, "than [the princes'] ... attachment to their mock majesty." But Mill went beyond eighteenth-century rationalism. He was an early "high modernist";[35] his life-long friend and colleague, Jeremy Bentham, had conceived of that icon of high modernism, the panopticon, the model prison that helped Foucault to theorize the power of surveillance and control that Mill thought would benefit India.

The contrast between Mill's and Tod's great historical texts, Mill's *History of British India* and Tod's *The Annals and Antiquities of Rajasthan*, the first a jeremiad against Indian religion and society, the second a panegyric for Rajput culture and society, highlight Mill's rationalist epistemology and view of human nature and Tod's romantic epistemology and view of human nature.[36] The 28-year-old Macauley's challenge in 1829 to James Mill's *Essay on Government* [1820], already an icon of the philosophical radicals,[37] illuminates the epistemological differences that underlie Tod's and Mill's parliamentary testimony in 1832. Mill argued that scientific theory must proceed from a finite set of assumptions about human nature, with the self- interest axiom at their center. From these one can deduce conclusions about the ways in which rational political actors can be expected to behave.[38] Tod would have agreed with Macauley when Macauley argued that "people act for all sorts of reasons, including—but by no means limited to—considerations of self interest."[39] Macauley like Tod takes a contextual, inductive approach to the study of history against Mill's abstract, deductive approach. According to Macauley "we learn more from 'experience' than from 'theory'." The "most pernicious" of Mill's assumptions for Macauley is that "men act always on the basis of self interest." This assumption, Macauley argued, "is either trivially true [because logically circular] or patently false; in either case it hardly suffices as a foundation upon which to erect an argument for ... a comprehensive theory of politics."[40]

Mill's testimony argued from *a priori* assumptions such as "we begin by taking the military power, and when we have taken that, we have taken all." Mill here adds another a priori assumption to the axiom that humans live by material self-interest, i.e. they can be governed by the fear that coercion generates, what Hobbes was referred to in his metaphor of the Leviathan and Indians referred to as *danda raj*.

Tod argued inductively, from experience, from empathetic understanding and from local knowledge. An example was his testimony about Company's new opium policy in Rajpootana:

> although in the treaties [of 1818] we expressly abjure internal interference, hardly had a state of repose succeeded the conflict of 1817–18, when, discovering that the chief agricultural product of Malwa and Lower Rajpootana was opium, which had progressively improved during the last 40 years, so as to compete with the Patna monopoly in the China market, we at once interposed, invading the rights of the native speculators, in order to appropriate their profits to ourselves. ... Monopoly in these regions produces a combination of evils; [it was] unjust, because we assumed fiscal powers in a country where our duties were simply protective; abolishing the impost and appropriating the transit duties, and deprived the local trader of a lucrative speculation: it was impolitic, because we diverted the efforts of the agricultural classes from the more important branches of husbandry; it was inquisitorial, because we not only sent circulars to chiefs, calling for a statement of the cultivation

of the plant, but despatched agents to the opium districts to make personal inspection and reports. To these political errors we may add the immoral tendency of the measure which led to every species of fraud. The gambling in opium was not surpassed by that of the London Stock Exchange; it seduced into speculation individuals of all ranks, from the prince to the scavenger, instances of both having come under my personal observation.

Notes

*   This chapter was previously published as "Tod vs Mill: Clashing Perspectives on British Rule in India and Indian Civilization: An Analysis Based on James Tod's and James Mill's 1832 Parliamentary Testimony," in Giles Tillotson, ed., *Tod's Rajasthan* (Mumbai: Marg Publications, 2007). Reprinted by permission.

1.   The transcription of Mill's oral testimony and Tod's testimony by letter make up Part II of this volume.

2.   Tod, like Sir William Jones and the eighteenth-century orientalists of the Asiatic Society of Bengal, viewed Indians as civilized in part because of Jones' claim that India's ancient language, Sanskrit, shared a common civilizational root, an "*ur*" or original Indo-European language, that provides a common linguistic ancestry for Sanskrit, Greek and other European languages. Tod and the orientalists associated language and people, an association that led Tod to believe that Indians shared common ancestors with Europeans. Tod's efforts to find Indian analogs to Greek and Roman god and heroes and his belief that Indians and Britons were distant cousins are

located in his participation in Jones' Indo-European languages paradigm.

For more about why the eighteenth-century orientalists of Bengal thought of India as civilized see our "Occidentalism and Orientalism ..." in S.C. Humphreys (ed.) *Cultures of Scholarship*, The Comparative Studies in Society and History Book Series (Ann Arbor, MI: University of Michigan Press, 1997), pp. 219–51.

3.   Uday Singh Mehta's *Liberalism and Empire* (Chicago: University of Chicago Press, 1999) shows how British liberals such as James Mill and John Stuart Mill squared the circle of affirming a Lockean liberal universalism, the doctrine that all humanity is the same, while declaring Indians to be different because they lacked civilization. Indians it seems were like infants and women, unfit to care for or improve themselves. As John Stuart Mill put it,

> Liberty, as a principle, has no application to any state of things anterior to the time when mankind has become capable of being improved. ... It is, perhaps, hardly necessary to say that his doctrine is meant to apply only to human beings in the maturity of their faculties. ... Those who are still in a state to require being taken care of by others, must be protected against their own actions as well as against external injury. John Stuart Mill, "On Liberty," in *Three Essays* (New York: Oxford University Press, 1975), p. 15.

Mehta invokes Edmund Burke to counter Mill's liberal universalism. In words that capture Tod's world view and objectives in writing *The Annals and Antiquities of Rajasthan*, Mehta argues that Burke's views contrast "starkly" with liberal universalism because of "the political and psychological significance he attaches to places. Individuals 'belong to,' 'come from,' and 'live in' places. For Burke, those philosophical emblems capture fundamental aspects of individual and collective identity. ... The normative force of history and location stem from their psychological centrality to identity formation." Mehta, *Liberalism and Empire*, 160–1.

4.   Terrence Ball, Introduction, *Mill*, p. xii.

5.   Here is how the anonymous author of a "Memoir of the Author" that proceeds Tod's posthumously published *Travels in Western India* (London: Wm. H. Allen and Co., 1839) put it: "Colonel Tod's father [the eldest son of Henry Tod and Janet Monteith, born 26th October 1745] was a native of Scotland, and descended from an ancient family, one of whose ancestors, John Tod, having rescued the children of Robert the Bruce, who were captives in England, was created by the King's own hand a knight banneret, with permission to bear the crest of a fox rampant [*Tod* being the name of a fox in Scotland], and the motto 'Vigilantia,' which is still borne by the family." P. xvii.

6.   Anonymous, "Memoir of the Author," *Travels*, footnote, p. xviii.

7.   The case for the enormous influence of Mill's *History of British India* on shaping India's image for successive generations of *raj* officials right down to Independence in 1947 can be found in Francis G. Hutchins, *The Illusion of Permanence: British Imperialism in India* (Princeton, N.J.: Princeton University Press, 1967). It is arguable that Mill's *History* is Edward Said's most telling example of "Orientalism." In his words: "What follows are schemes for ... reconstituting [the natives] as people requiring a European presence. ... Kipling's fiction [posited] the Indian as a creature clearly needing British tuteledge ... since without Britain India would disappear into its own corruption and underdevelopment. [Kipling here repeats the well-known views

of James and John Stuart Mill ... during their tenure at India House]."
Edward W. Said, *Culture and Imperialism* (New York: Vintage Books,
1994), p. 167.

8.   We use the term *longue duree* in the popular sense of "the long
perspective" and not in the way that the originator of the term,
Fernand Braudel, preferred it to be used. For an intellectual history
of Braudel that makes clear how Braudel used the term and why he
invented it see Oswyn Murray's introduction to Braudel's *Memory and
the Mediterranean* (New York: Alfred Knopf, 2001).

9.   See Renato Resaldo, "Culture Visibility and Invisibility," in his
article mentioned Ryerson lecture and in "Engaging Subjective
Knowledge ..." in his *Culture and Truth: The Remaking of Social Analysis*
(Boston: Beacon Press, 1989). We have reversed Resaldo's insight about
"the natives" gaining power after decolonization and independence,
"the more power one has, the less culture one enjoys, and the more
culture one has, the less power one wields," pp. 198–204.

10.   Although little noticed and heralded by fellow scholars of the
Asiatic Society's orientalist learning, James Tod was an active partici-
pant in it by, *inter alia*, launching the study of numismatics in India.
While in Mewar Tod amassed a collection of 20,000 coins, arranged
them in broad groups and commented on the categories he had created. He was able to document the main dynasties "from the time of
the Guptas right up till the Mohammeden conquests. Indeed, India's
medieval history has since been largely constructed on the basis of
numismatics." John Keay, *India Discovered: The Recovery of a Lost
Civilization* (London: Harper-Collins, 2001), p. 87.

For an account of Tod's connection to Romanticism including his
relationship to the scholarship of Henry Hallam on the feudalism of

medieval Europe and the historical novels of Sir Walter Scott see Chapter 1.

11.   Mill's world view arose from his close relationship to Jeremy Bentham and his long-term involvement with Bentham's Utilitarian philosophy and from his roots in Scotland's Evangelical religious revival.

12.   Hutchins, *The Illusion of Permanence*; Mehta, *Liberalism and Empire*; Ronald B. Inden, *Imagining India* (Cambridge, MA.: Basil Blackwell, 1990).

13.   In 1835 Bentinck's Council agreed to allocate its educational funds to teaching western learning to young Indians in the English language. Macauley's minute, adopted on March 7, 1835, stated that in higher education the Company's goal should be the promotion of European science and literature among the natives of India. All funds appropriated for purposes of education were to be employed on English education alone. Macaulay's project of Anglicized uniformity was deepened in 1857 when Sir Charles Wood's 1854 Education Dispatch recommending, *inter alia*, the establishment of English medium universities in the three presidencies—Bengal, Madras, and Bombay—was acted upon.

The Macauley quotes can be found in Surjit Mansingh, *Historical Dictionary of India* (New Delhi: Vision Books, 2003), p. 236.

14.   Eric Stokes, *The English Utilitarians and India* (Oxford: The Clarendon Press, 1959).

15.   Duff had accepted an offer made by the foreign mission committee of the Free Church's general assembly to become its first missionary to India. Ordained in August 1829, he left at once for India. Reaching Calcutta in May 1830, he identified himself with a policy which had far-reaching results, converting high-caste Hindus

and high-status Muslims. Up to this time Protestant missions in India had succeeded in converting low-castes and untouchables. Duff saw that to reach high-status communities education must take the place of evangelizing methods. He succeeded in altering Company policy and in securing the recognition of education as a missionary activity by Christian churches in Britain.

His English-medium school put the Bible at the center of a curriculum that included a broad range of secular knowledge. English was used because it was to be the language of higher education in India and the means to give primacy to Western knowledge. Duff's school soon became a missionary college.

In 1844 Duff helped to found the *Calcutta Review* and served as its Editor from 1845 to 1849 when he returned home. In 1856 he returned to India in time to witness the 1857 rebellion. His descriptive letters were collected in a volume entitled *The Indian Mutiny: Its Causes and Results* [1858].

16. As cited at p. 113 of *Postmodern Gandhi and Other Essays: Gandhi in the World and at Home* (New Delhi: Oxford University Press, 2006).

Charles Grant could not "… avoid recognizing in the people of Indostan a race of men lamentably degenerate and base," and John Stuart Mill, echoing the view of his father, James Mill, regretted that "in truth, the Hindu, like the eunuch, excels in the qualities of the slave." See Sita Ram Goel's letter to the *Times of India*, March 2, 1988 for these familiar quotes. Macauley too found Hinduism abominable. As he told the House of Commons:

"In no part of the world has a religion ever existed more unfavourable to the moral and intellectual health of our race. The Brahminical mythology is so absurd that it necessarily debases every mind which receives it as truth; and with this absurd mythology is bound up an absurd system of physics, an absurd geography, an absurd astronomy. ... All is hideous, and grotesque and ignoble. As this superstition is of all superstitions the most irrational, and of all superstitions the most inelegant, so it is of all superstitions the most immoral." As quoted in Keay, *India Discovered*, p. 78.

17.   The story of cartridges greased with animal fat that had to be readied by mouth whether of pig that offended Muslims or cow that offended Hindus is probably the most frequently cited source of dishonor. Serving overseas also violated traditional norms.

18.   For analyses of the East India Company's annexation policy and practice see Michael H. Fisher, ed., *The Politics of the British Annexation of India, 1757–1857* (Delhi: Oxford University Press, 1993).

19.   According to Surjit Mansingh's summary of the literature on 1857, "there was no unity of purpose, much less a unified command structure or common strategy among the Indians; they fought for sectional, parochial, or personal objectives against the one common enemy, British rule." Surjit Mansingh, *Historical Dictionary of India* (New Delhi: Vision Books, 1999), pp. 427–428.

20.   The 1857 rebellion had many causes and reasons. Not least were the policies and actions of the East India Company's penultimate Governor-General, the Marquess of Dalhousie [1848–1856]. He engaged in extensive conquests [e.g. Punjab] and, via the doctrine of lapse, numerous "annexations." He enormously increased Company direct rule but created the conditions for its demise. His annexation in 1856 of Awadh, bastion of Mughal culture and symbolic of the Company's system of shared sovereignty, sent a "frisson of fear" to Indian rulers. Who would be next?

21.   Queen Victoria's Proclamation is available in C.H. Philips, *The Evolution of India and Pakistan, 1858 to 1947: Select Documents* (London: Oxford University Press, 1962), pp. 10–11.

22.   The East India Company's first charter giving it exclusive trading rights with India was granted by Queen Elizabeth in 1600. A Regulating Act in 1773 established parliamentary control over the Company in order to deal with its by-then immense domestic financial and political power as well as its growing political power in India. The Charter Act of 1813, *inter alia*, declared British sovereignty over territories captured in India. The 1833 Act that followed Tod's and Mill's testimony, *inter alia*, empowered the Governor General in Council to legislate for all persons residing in British India.

23.   Tod distinguished in his Parliamentary testimony between the "predatory system" of the Mahrattas and the rulers of Rajpootana's ancient kingdoms.

24.   Tod and Mill were, in a sense, polar opposites on the question of the nature and value of British rule in India. In their time, there were renowned Company servants who took middling positions between them. The most well known at the time and subsequently, perhaps as an artifact of scholarship about them, are John Shore, Thomas Monro, Monstuart Elphinstone, John Malcolm, and Charles Metcalf. We note that James Tod seems to have been regarded as a lesser figure during his time and was not included in post-colonial scholarly works such as Phililp Woodruff's book cited below.

Mill in his testimony defers to but disagrees with John Malcom:

> But what is of chief importance is duly to estimate an opinion maintained by persons of high name, whose opinions deserve the greatest attention, (among others Sir John Malcolm) ... [He holds] the

opinion that we ought to endeavour to retain this intermediate state as long as it is possible. From the view which I take of the matter, my opinion (of little weight, indeed, compared with that of Sir John Malcolm), cannot but be, that *the more speedily we [abandon subsidiary alliances] ... the better.*

Despite his equivocation Mill's questioner took his meaning: "You may then almost be considered to say, that India has been conquered and administered in spite of instructions from England?"

Tod cites Sir Thomas Munro ["one of the most practical of our own politicians"] as sharing his concern that, despite official policy and denials, the ultimate effect of Company rule will be, as Mill advocates in his testimony, the elimination of Indian rulers and direct rule over the whole of the subcontinent.

Surjit Mansingh distinguishes three positions among the leading Company administrator:

[1] Some men, known as Orientalists, respected Indian traditions and institutions, saw the danger of hasty innovations, and held their primary duty to be maintenance and restoration until such time as Indian society had recovered, so to speak, from its evident torpor. [2] Another group of men, including William Bentinck and Thomas Macaulay, were radicals with a belief in reason and in progress, who advocated bold innovation to redeem a moribund Eastern society through Western wisdom. [3] Elphinstone belonged to third group, liberal conservative in attitude, which saw the desirability of introducing some Western ideas and values while convinced of the strength of traditional Indian institutions and looked to an eventual integration of the two. Mansingh's *Historical Dictionary*, pp. 134–5.

See also Volume One, *The Founders*, of Philip Woodruff's two volume, *The Men Who Ruled India* (New York: St. Martins Press, 1953, 1954) for John Shore and other EIC luminaries.

25. All quotes from Tod's testimony are from James Tod, "Testimony to Parliament, Reports from Committees, Session 6 December 1831–16 August 1832, Appendix 13, Letter from Lieut. Col. Tod to T.H. Villiers, Esq., *Minutes of Evidence taken before the Select Committee on the Affairs of the East India Company, VI. Political or Foreign [Vol. VII]. Vol. XIV.* (London: House of Commons, Parliament of England, 1832), pp. 122–35, reproduced in Part II of this volume.

26. All quotes from Mill's testimony are from James Mill, "Testimony to Parliament 16 February 1832, The Right Hon. Sir James MacIntosh, in the Chair, Reports from Committees, Session 6 December 1831–16 August 1832."*Minutes of Evidence Taken before the Select Committee on the Affairs of the East India Company, VI. Political or Foreign [Vol. VII]. Vol XIV* (London: House of Commons, Parliament of England, 1832), pp 3–10, reproduced in Part II of this volume.

27. Tod wrote to the Committee that

The treaties with the Rajpoot States differ from all our former engagements in this important point, that there is no mention of *subsidiary* alliance; and the tribute which we draw from them, though galling in a financial point of view, has none of the odium that attached to paying for a force which, under the name of protection from external danger, was in fact a degrading check upon themselves.

28. We have of late heard much of a Russian invasion. The progressive advance of this colossal power in Central Asia is well known; its influence from Bokhara to Lahore; and it is against this

influence that we have to guard. Its constant exercise answers all the purposes of a state of actual hostility, by its operation on our finances. A Russian invasion, however, must be a work of time; the plans of Russia must be matured in Central Asia, where she must establish her power before she can hope for successful aggression; though whether the *Dowranis* could be brought to exchange their barbarous independence for Russian despotism, may be doubted.

29.   Tod goes on to admonish and warn those who, like James Mill, despise Indian rulers and want them removed as soon as possible. His claim that 50,000 Rajputs "would die in our defence" "... is asserted from a thorough knowledge of their [the Rajputs'] character and history.

"The Rajpoots want no change; they only desire the recognition and inviolability of their independence; but we must bear in mind, that mere parchment obligations are good for little in the hour of danger. It is for others to decide whether they will sap the foundation of our rule by a passive indifference to the feelings of this race or whether, by acts of kindness, generosity, and politic forbearance, they will ensure the exertion of all their moral and physical energies in one common cause with us."

In his *Annals* he had recently spelled out what he had in mind.

"To combine the Rajpoot states in a federal union, of which the British Government constituted itself protector, had long been looked upon by the wisest of our Governors-General, as a *desideratum*. Such an union was justly regarded as a consolidation of the elements of fixed government against that predatory system [of the Mahrattas] which had so long disorganized India;

and having achieved this by a policy which secures to us not only their military resources but the control of all their political relations, (and this with the least possible degree of evil) we have not only checked that system, but have raised a barrier of the most powerful kind against invasion."

30.   Burke emphasized the importance for liberty [as opposed to tyranny] of a hereditary aristocracy whose rights were prescribed by an ancient constitution and that the circumstances and, with respect to India, that habits of every country are to decide upon the form of its government. See J.G.A. Pocock's Introduction to Edmund Burke, *Reflections on the Revolution in France* (Indianapolis, IN.: Hackett Publishing Company, 1987).

Tod here opposes Mill's version of "Oriental despotism" with an argument that turns Montesquieu's explanation for oriental despotism on its head. "Montesquieu," Perry Anderson tells us, "... inherited from his predecessors the basic axioms that Asiatic States lacked stable private property or a hereditary nobility ['intermediary powers' in relation to checking absolutism in France] and were therefore arbitrary and tyrannical." Perry Anderson, 'The Asiatic Mode of Production,' in *Lineages of the Absolute State* (London: NLB, 1977), pp. 463–4.

31.   See Letter of expatriated Chiefs of Marwar to the British Political Agent, tracing all their sufferings to the alliance. The *Annals*, Vol. 1, p. 197.

32.   Terence Ball tells us that Mill "harbored ... an abiding hatred for an hereditary aristocracy." Terence Ball (ed.), *James Mill. Political Writings*. Cambridge Texts in the History of Political Thought (Cambridge, UK: Cambridge University Press, 1992), p. xiv.

33. "In all those feudal principalities," Tod wrote to the Committee, "the rights of the princes and their vassals are co-eval, being all, in fact, members of one great patriarchial family," which enjoins us "to guard the well-defined rights and privileges of the feudatories against the abuse of authority."

34. From Epistle III. "Of the Nature and State of Man with respect to Society," in Alexander Pope, *Essay on Man.* http://www. theotherpages.org/poems/pope-i.html Transcribed by hand from The Complete Poetical Works of Alexander Pope, Student's Cambridge Edition, Houghton Mifflin Company, 1903 (edited by H.W. Boynton). [The first two Epistles were written in 1732, the third in 1733, and the fourth in 1744].

35. For how the term "high modernism" captures the outlook of James Mill see James C. Scott, *Seeing Like a State: How Certain Schemes to Improve the Human Condition Have Failed* (New Haven: Yale University Press, 1998), especially Introduction and Chapter 9, "Thin Simplifications and Practical Knowledge: Metis," and James C. Scott, "High Modernist Social Engineering: The Case of the Tennessee Valley Authority," in Lloyd I. Rudolph and John Kurt Jacobsen (eds.), *Experiencing the State* (New Delhi and New York: Oxford University Press, 2006).

36. For an elaboration of Tod's Romantic epistemology and view of human nature see Chapter 1. "We find," we wrote, "that his interpretation [in the *Annals*] was animated by three related metaphors or models, medieval feudalism, romantic nationalism and civilizational progress," p. 10.

37. We are about to show how Mill and Macauley disagreed about epistemology in ways that highlight differences between Mill

and Tod. The Mill–Macauley controversy did not prevent Macauley from following Mill's views in the *History of British India* about the degraded nature of Hinduism. See *supra*.

38. Brian Berry and Alan Ryan read Mill as the original proponent of rational choice thinking, analysis and explanation. See Terrence Ball, *Mill*, pp. xxvi–xxvii.

39. Ball, *Mill*, p. xxvii.

40. Ball, *Mill*, p. xxiv.

3   Tod and Vernacular History

James Tod's *The Annals and Antiquities of Rajasthan* had a formidable influence on nationalist, imperial, and Rajasthan history and historiography. Less noticed has been his contribution to the writing of vernacular history. In this chapter we discuss how Tod's *The Annals and Antiquities of Rajasthan* (Vol. 1, 1829; Vol. 2, 1832)[1] contributed to the writing of vernacular history and how vernacular history shaped Indian historiography, history, and identity.

What does the term "vernacular history" connote? Broadly, it suggests people's history or common man's history as opposed to academic history. Academic history is a conceptual invention with a career, institutions, and an organized body of practitioners.[2] Vernacular history is the common man's history in two senses—the language through which it is expressed and the sources on which it is based. Its language is everyday local language, not theoretical, specialized, or academic language. Its sources are not those of academic history, archival records, and foundational texts, but those found in folk and traditional forms of expression and performance such as ballads, poems, stories and recitations, and, more recently, in popular media such as television, film, and, as we shall see, in the form of the Amar Chitra Katha, the popular series that presents in comic book form the great Indian epics, mythology, history, folklore, and fables.[3]

We first became aware of Tod and his influence on what we would later recognize as vernacular history in 1984 when, on a visit to Calcutta, as it was then known, we spent several hours talking to the doyen of Bengali historians and cultural critics, Barun De. He told us about how as an 11-year-old he learned about Rajput heroes and stories by reading Robert Payne's summary of Tod which was sold as a textbook in the bazaar. In 1969, the late Nurul Hassan, the Mughal historian and erstwhile Congress minister for education, told De that most Bengalis wanted to be Rajputs. De spoke at length about Tod's influence on Bengali poetry (including that of Rabindranath Tagore),[4] plays, novels, and songs.

More recently, Shail Mayaram has argued that "few persons have had the kind of impact on the Indian popular nationalist imagination that James Tod [1782–1835] has had.... He was among the first scholars who shifted Orientalist interests from the classical to the vernacular, from the written to oral traditions, from the brahman to the bard."[5]

Tod himself presents a systematic account of his sources for writing the *Annals* in his "Author's Introduction" to Volume I:[6]

> In the absence of regular and legitimate historical records, there are, however, other native works ... which in the hands of a skilful and patient investigator, would afford no despicable materials for the history of India. The first of these are the *purans* and genealogical legends of the princes, which, obscured as they are by mythological details, allegory, and improbable circumstances, contain many facts that serve as beacons to direct research of the historian.

Tod continues:

> The heroic poems of India constitute another resource for history. *Bards may be regarded as the primitive historians of mankind* [emphasis added].... The functions of the bard were doubtless employed in recording real events and in commemorating real personages.... The poets are the chief, though not the sole, historians of Western India."[7]

Inattention to vernacular history may help to explain why standard histories of India such as those by Stanley Wolpert,[8] Hermann Kulke and Dietmar Rothermund,[9] Burton Stein,[10] Bernard S. Cohn,[11] Sugata Bose and Ayesha Jalal,[12] and Barbara D. Metcalf and Thomas R. Metcalf[13] do not mention or source Tod's *Annals*. Another reason for historians of modern India to ignore Tod may be because he was perceived as writing about "princely India," India's old regime, a subject regarded as so hopelessly anachronistic, so much an ornamentalist sideshow,[14] as not to be worthy of attention by most post-independence historians of India. Rajasthan's identification with princely India may help to explain how even Philip Woodruff in *The Founders*, the first volume of *The Men Who Ruled India*, a book that celebrates the bigger-than-life personalities of the East India Company's direct rule such as John Shore, Thomas Monro, Mountstuart Elphinstone, and Charles Metcalfe, does not mention James Tod even though he served the East India Company for 24 years from 1799 to 1823.[15]

The one exception to historians of India overlooking Tod is Percival Spear. In *A History of India*, volume 2, he argues that a post-Macaulay "new class" of English-educated Indians "found means to support their self-respect in works of Europeans glorifying the history and cultural achievements of the Indian past. ... Tod's *Annals of Rajasthan*, celebrating the deeds of Rajput chivalry ... became a bestseller in pirate editions in nineteenth century India."[16]

It has been left to John Keay, a non-academic, "popular" historian who has written about the East India Company[17] and its orientalists[18] (of whom Tod was one) to use Tod's *Annals* to characterize and interpret Indian history in his *India: A History*.[19] Unlike Philip Woodruff, Keay counts Tod (in Rajasthan) along with Colin McKenzie and Thomas Munro (in the south), John Malcolm (in central India), Mountstuart

Elphinstone and James Grant Duff (in Maharashtra), and John Shore (in United Provinces [Uttar Pradesh]) as among the scholar-administrators who tried to "govern India in accordance with its own customs and so win the approbation of the governed."[20] And unlike the standard histories of India, Keay uses Tod's history to bring the Rajputs into the narratives of Indian history from Prithvi Raj in the late twelfth century through the Mughal, Maratha, and East India Company eras.[21]

The hermeneutic of viewing Indian history and culture through a vernacular lens was strengthened in 2006 when Sheldon Pollock published his much awaited *The Language of the Gods in the World of Men: Sanskrit, Culture, and Power in Premodern India*.[22] Pollock argues that the adoption of Sanskrit, the language of ritual and liturgy, in worldly public documents, a process that started around the beginning of the Common Era, was followed at the end of the first millennium by the gradual replacement of Sanskrit by local vernacular languages. The introduction of Sanskrit and its subsequent challenge by the vernaculars in public documents and worldly literature was politically motivated in that Sanskrit expressed efforts by rulers to be cosmopolitans, not locals, and the use of the vernaculars expressed the desire of local elites to affirm their regions, to be regarded as sons of the soil.[23]

Another recent entrant into the discourse about vernacular history is a book edited by Raziuddin Aquil and Partha Chatterjee, *History in the Vernacular*. Here is how the editors make their case for non-academic pre-colonial regional history as vernacular history:[24]

> Looking closely at vernacular contexts and traditions of historical production, this book questions the assumption that there was no history writing in India before colonialism. It suggests that careful readings reveal distinctly indigenous historical narratives. These narratives may be embedded within non-historical literary genres, such as poems, ballads, and works within the itihasa-purana tradition, *but they are marked by discursive signs that allow them to be recognized as historical* [emphasis added].
>
> Vernacular history traditions in Assam, Bengal, the North-East, Kerala, the Andhra-Tamil region, Maharashtras, and Uttar Pradesh are examined, all be it noted, in non-princely or British ruled parts of India.

The many bardic sources, not to mention the *bhai*s (government books), *khyats* (chronicles celebrating the histories of states) and inscriptions used by James Tod in researching and writing the *Annals*, do not find a place in the Aquil and Chatterjee volume on pre-colonial regional "history in the vernacular." We can only speculate about why this is so. One reason may be that progressive historians have assigned princely India to the dustbin of history. This despite the fact, as we shall see below, that Tod's Rajput history and Rajput heroes and heroines played a major role in shaping the imagination of early nationalist thought in Bengal and subsequently more broadly in providing the source for nationalist history and Indian identity. In contemporary India, Tod's narratives, *inter alia*, of Prithvi Raj, Padmini, and Rana Pratap have been featured in *Amar Chitra Katha*.

Let us turn first to how Tod's *Annals* shaped the first phase of Indian nationalism in Bengal. Much has been written on this subject but for our purposes today we want to rely on the late Meenaskhi Mukherjee's last book, *An Indian for All Seasons: The Many Lives of R. C. Dutt*.[25] In that book she shows how the Bengali novels of R.C. Dutt shaped a vernacular view of Indian history and identity. Of his six novels in Bengali, two—*Dawn over Maharashtra* (1878) and *The Sunset of the Rajputs* (1879)— belong to the genre of historical fiction, a genre more or less invented by Sir Walter Scott whom Dutt admired and sought to emulate. Dutt gives his reason for writing historical fiction in an "authorial digression" in *Dawn over Maharashtra*: "Reader," he writes, "I have taken up the pen only in the hope that we can sit together to sing of our nation's glory and remember the bravery of the past."[26]

Mukherjee tells us that it was important for Dutt "to construct a heroic and martial heritage in order to counteract the image of the weak and effeminate India which the British have been perpetuating."[27] James Mill, whose *The History of India* (1817) was compulsory reading for Englishmen coming to serve in India, "categorically stated that the [Hindus] possess a certain softness both of their person and address that distinguish them from the manlier races of Europe." Before Mill, Richard Orme had opined that "all natives of India showed an effeminacy of character, but the Bengalis were of still weaker frame and more enervated nature."[28] Later, after the 1857 rebellion and Victoria's 1858 Declaration replacing the East India Company with direct rule, the stereotype of the effeminate Hindu was replaced by the stereotype of the masculine martial races, the Sikhs, Pathans, Rajputs, and Muslims, and the feminine non-martial races of whom the Bengalis, whom the British knew longest and best, remained the leading exemplars.[29]

James Tod was the exception to British authors who maligned Indians by projecting them as weak and effeminate. Tod's image of the martial Rajput preceded by a generation or more the theory of the masculine martial and feminine non-martial races that became central to the Raj discourse after the 1857 rebellion and remained influential during the late colonial and post-independence eras.

Tod's *The Annals and Antiquities of Rajasthan* "became a source book for many historical novels and plays in various Indian languages."[30] "Tod's romantic presentation of Rajput valour," Mukherjee writes, "appealed to the nationalist imagination of many writers of the time, and Romesh Chunder Dutt was one of them."[31] In several footnotes in his novels, Dutt acknowledges Tod's book as his inspiration. There is one figure who rose above the various conflicts in Dutt's historical novels and that figure was the Rana Pratap of Tod's creation. He is depicted as "almost mythical in stature, a perfect embodiment of the physical prowess of a Kshatriya combined with the austerity and self-discipline of a Brahmin."³² Mukherjee quotes from Dutt's *The Sunset of the Rajputs*:

> He had vowed to sleep on the ground on the bare grass until Chittor's freedom was restored. As long as the mission remained unfilled, he had resolved never to touch gold or silver. Even the sages of the past did not perform the kind of austerities that Pratap Singh did for achieving his goal" (*Rajput Jivan Sandhya*, p. 263).³³

Mukherjee tells us that Rana Pratap is the hero that Tod iconized in his *Annals*. In support of his admiration for Rana Pratap, Dutt used an excerpt from a two-page-long footnote from Tod's *Annals*:

> Had Mewar possessed its Thucidides or her Xenophon, neither the wars of the Peloponesus or the retreat of the 'ten thousand' would have yielded more diversified incident than the historic Mewar.... There is not a pass in the alpine Aravali that is not sanctified by some deed of Pratap. Some brilliant victory or glorious defeat. Haldighat is the Thermopylae of Mewar, the field of Deweir her Marathon. (p. 295)

Mukherjee concludes her discussion of Dutt's construction of Tod by telling us that "Tod's metonymic evocation of Greece as the signifier for the whole of Europe" is parallel to Dutt's appropriation of Rajasthan into the narrative of Bengal and the projection of Bengal as synonymous with the whole of India.³⁴

Tod's image of the martial Rajput reached well beyond Bengali nationalism's search for martial heroes and anti-imperialist freedom fighters to Mahatma Gandhi, the pre-eminent leader of Indian nationalism. Tod's use of the Thermopylae trope caught Gandhi's attention. Tod invoked Thermopylae in the large and in the small: in the large by analogizing Rana Pratap's battle with Akbar's army at Haldighati, a defilade like that at Thermopylae, and in the small by remarking, "There is not a petty State in Rajasthan that has not had its Thermopylae."[35] In 1920, just five years after his return to India from 21 years in South Africa, Gandhi told members of a Hindu audience at the Law College in Madras fearful of Muslim martial traditions that they too could call on a legacy of bravery and courage. Colonel Tod, Gandhi told them, had said that India was "dotted with a thousand Thermopaelies [sic]."[36]

Gandhi's use of Tod was capped by his invocation of him to convince participants at the momentous Second Round Table Conference in London in 1931 that India was capable of defending itself. It would have defense forces and it had martial races to man them.

There is all the material there ... Mohammedans ... Sikhs ... the Gurkha.... Then there are the Rajputs, who are supposed to be responsible for a thousand Thermopylaes, and not one little Thermopylae.... That is what the Englishman, Colonel Tod, told us. Colonel Tod has taught us to believe that every pass in Rajputana is a

Thermopylae. Do these people stand in need of learning
the art of defense?[37]

Tod's view of Rajput history and images of Rajput heroes
continued to shape the meaning and consequences of vernacular history after independence in a new print media, the *Amar
Chitra Katha*, the comic books that shaped the perceptions and
attitudes of several recent generations of young Indians.
Nandani Chandra's *The Classic Popular Amar Chitra Katha,
1967–2007* shows us how and why this happened. She details
how the *Amar Chitra Katha* uses Tod's *Annals* to construct a
version of Indian historiography and national identity. She
speaks of a "Rajput dominated history of anti-imperialism."[38]
The Rajputs, Chandra tells us, are naturalized as Kshatriyas
and their martial valor is useful "in countering the colonial
construct of the effete Hindu."[39] Hindu identity, she continues, was that of a martial race as embodied particularly by
the Rajput.[40]

Chandra illustrates her argument by analyzing the seven
opening frames of a *katha* (story) about Rana Pratap, whose
story originates in Tod's *Annals*. "The comic," she says,
"presents us with a history of Rajputs to demonstrate their
role as the indefatigable guardians of India since time
immemorial." The text says that they have risen "to defend
our motherland every time there has been a foreign invasion, be it the Greeks, the Khaljis, the Slave dynasty, the
Mughals or the British."[41]

"The comic begins," Chandra tells us,

> with seven cameo shots of the history of Chittor before
> panning to the hero Rana Pratap and his mission to free
> Chittor from the Mughal yoke. The first frame covers
> the entire page. It is a close up of what is presumably the
> Rajput archtype, an ancient guard looking the reader
> straight in the eye. His *pagdi* [turban], a flamboyant white
> beard combed [in the Mewar manner] on either side with
> a parting in the middle, the U-shaped tilak on the large
> forehead identical to that of a Vaishnav devotee's, the
> spear and the shield, all convey the message that as long as
> this man stands guard, the fort stretching out behind him
> will remain safe.[42]

In conclusion, we want to look to the future of vernacular
history in television and film. Starting with the 1986 78-episode
Ramayana television series[43] followed by many subsequent historical "blockbuster" series and innumerable Bollywood historical[44]
films, and the internationally and domestically influential
Richard Attenborough film *Gandhi* (1983),[45] media-driven vernacular history has increasingly shaped the meaning and consequences of history in the public sphere. In media-saturated
democracies such as India and the United States, vernacular
history has moved from the world of history books (where it
still plays a role) to the world of the public sphere and politics,
where it becomes a ground for promoting and contesting identity and ideology.

Notes

1.   We are working with the two-volume edition by Rupa & Co. (New Delhi, 1997). The first edition was published by Routledge and Kegan Paul Ltd (London, 1829).

2.   The view that history is a conceptual invention and an organized body of knowledge with self-conscious practitioners has been challenged by Daniel Woolf in *A Global History of History* (Cambridge: Cambridge University Press, 2011). Woolf distinguishes between History (capitalized) and history (lower case), the former an agent that in a Hegelian manner makes things happen in time and space, and the latter literary or non-literary representations of events, persons, or ideas about the past. Jonathan Clark in a review of Woolf's book in *The Times Literary Supplement* of May 13, 2011 mocks Woolf's view that history is natural, present everywhere and always, by invoking Cole Porter's "Let's Fall in Love": "Birds do it. Bees do it ... even educated fleas do it."

Woolf confuses matters by mentioning that in "modern times" lowercase history can also refer to "a professional discipline." But he fails to recognize adequately that history is itself a conceptual formation with its own history, practitioners, institutions, and regulating mechanisms. In what follows we distinguish vernacular history from academic history, history as a concept with its own intellectual history as a professional discipline.

3.   Before launching on an analysis of how Tod helped to create vernacular history and how his *Annals* contributed to the creation of vernacular history we want to enter a caveat. We are not entering into how Tod's vernacular history may have contributed to

buttressing colonial rule, as some Saideans suggest, or to communal ideology.

4.   Ironically, when Tagore, near the end of his life in 1937 (he died in 1941), encountered the real Rajasthan on a visit there, he was completely disillusioned. In *Rajputana*, he expressed this disillusionment in a poem he wrote in Bengali (translated for us by the late Sujit Mukherjee) soon after his visit. We quote here its opening lines:

> This is a portrait of Rajputana./To me it looks/like the intolerable burden/Continuing to live humped on the back of death./This search of a witless past/to find its meaning in a wayward present/and its rights lost in some void./See that hill-top fort/enclosing its meaningless frown,/see the victory tower/raising its angry fist against an adverse fate./Death clutched on long ago/yet it does not know how to die/hence it must suffer humiliation/night and day/at the hands of out-of-turn time.

5.   Shail Mayaram, "The Magic of Prithviraj, Padmini and Pratap in the Vernacular Imaginaire: Revising the Interface of Colonialism, Orientalism, and Nationalism," International Centre Occasional Publication 3, p. 2.

Mayaram's article includes seriatim listings of how Tod influenced historical and more recent writing about Prithviraj (pp. 8–12), Padmini (pp. 12–16), and Pratap (pp. 16–19). Apparently she was unable to consider Cynthia Talbot's critique of Tod's use of the *Prithvi Raj Raso*, "Contesting Knowledges in Colonial India: The Question of *Prithviraj Raso's* Historicity", in Cynthia Talbot (ed.), *Knowing India: Colonial and Modern Constructions of the Past* (Delhi: Yoda Press, 2011), pp. 171–212, or Ramya Sreenivasan's use of Tod in her study of the Padmini story, *The Many Lives of a Rajput Queen:*

Heroic Pasts in India, c. 1500–1900. (Seattle: University of Washington Press, 2007).

6.   Tod, *The Annals and Antiquities of Rajasthan*, pp. xiii–xx.

7.   Tod, *Annals*, p. xv. Tod goes on to mention other non-vernacular sources of history, "the accounts given by the Brahmins of the endowments of the temples ... which furnish occasions for the introduction of historical and chronological details.... The controversies of the Jains furnish much historical information.... From a close and attentive examination of Jain records ... many chasms in Hindu history might be filled up" (Tod, *Annals*, pp. xvi–xvii). Finally, Tod mentions "inscriptions 'cut on the rock,' coins, copper-plate grants, containing charters of immunities, and expressing many singular features of civil government, constitute ... materials for the historian" (Tod, *Annals*, p. xvii).

8.   Stanley Wolpert, *A New History of India* (New York: Oxford University Press, 2000).

9.   Hermann Kulke and Dietmar Rothermund, *A History of India* (London and New York: Routledge, 1998).

10.   Burton Stein, *A History of India* (New Delhi: Oxford University Press, 2001).

11.   Bernard S. Cohn, *Colonialism and Its Forms of Knowledge: The British in India* (Princeton, NJ: Princeton University Press, 1996).

12.   Sugata Bose and Ayesha Jalal, *Modern South Asia: History, Culture, Political Economy*, Second Edition (New York and London: Routledge, 2004). It is not quite the case that Bose and Jalal do not mention Tod. They do but in the curious context of arguing that the British Raj tried to settle the countryside "by lending support to principles of hierarchy and ritual distinctions.... One of the better known

products of this enterprise is James Tod's *The Annals and Antiquities of Rajasthan*, compiled [sic] between 1829 and 1832."

13.   Barbara D. Metcalf and Thomas R. Metcalf, *A Concise History of Modern India, Second Edition* (Cambridge: Cambridge University Press, 2006).

14.   For the concept of ornamentalism in imperial history and rule, see David Cannadine, *Ornamentalism: How the British Saw Their Empire* (Oxford and New York: Oxford University Press, 2001).

15.   Tod does get a mention in Woodruff's bibliography of Part III, *The Golden Age, 1798–1858* as "Tod: Annals of Rajasthan."

16.   Thomas George Percival Spear, *A History of India, Vol. 2* (Hammondsworth: Penguin Books, 1965).

17.   John Keay, *The Honourable Company: A History of the English East India Company* (London: Harper Collins, 1991).

18.   John Keay, *India Discovered* (London: Collins, 1988).

19.   John Keay, *India: A History* (London: Harper Collins, 2000).

20.   Keay, *India: A History*, p. 426.

21.   For example, Keay tells us that while Tod was "mistaken in taking Chand's 'poetical histories' as reliable evidence ... Tod did both history and Indian nationalism a useful service ... [by] rehabilitating Prithviraj as also the *kshatriya* dynasties of Rajasthan" (Keay, *India: A History*, p. 233).

22.   Sheldon Pollock, *The Language of the Gods in the World Men: Sanskrit, Culture, and Power in Premodern India* (Berkeley and Los Angeles: University of California Press, 2006).

23.   Our understanding of Pollock's argument is based in part on an extended appreciative but critical review of *The Language of the Gods in the World of Men* by Herman Tieken, "The Process of

Vernacularization in South Asia," *Journal of the Economic and Social History of the Orient* 51 (2008): 338–83.

Tieken concludes his review by observing:

> The process of vernacularization in India was clearly not a matter of the vernaculars replacing a dominant literary culture but rather of finding a place for themselves within that literary culture. As we have seen, in the eighth century Kannada was called a Prakrit and around the same time Tamil was assigned the role of a Prakrit or Apabhramsa. Moreover, during the almost entire second millennium the North Indian vernaculars were gathered together, albeit implicitly, under the category of Apabhramsa. On closer consideration the process of vernacularization may thus be characterized as a form of Sanskritization, with the vernaculars taking on the cloak of Prakrit or Apabhramsa.... Despite the fact that an Apabhramsa is supposed to represent a regional language, the inclusion of a regional language into the category of Apabhramsa almost automatically blurs, not denies, its connection with a specific region. In this respect the Prakrits and Apabhramsa[s] partake of the translocal character of Sanskrit.... It would seem that each of these literary languages in its own way tried to avoid the impression of being connected with only one specific dialect of the regional language concerned. They are "little" Sanskrits, doing what Sanskrit does, on a local or smaller scale. (p. 379)

24. Raziuddin Aquil and Partha Chatterjee (eds.), *History in the Vernacular* (New Delhi: Permanent Black, 2008).

25. Meenakshi Mukherjee, *"An Indian for All Seasons": The Many Lives of R.C. Dutt* (New Delhi: Penguin, 2009).

26. Mukherjee, *Dutt*, p. 226.

27. Mukherjee, *Dutt*, p. 226.

28. Mukherjee, *Dutt*, p. 226.

29. For a discussion on the sources, context, and consequences of the distinction between masculine and feminine races in India, see Lloyd I. Rudolph and Susanne Hoeber Rudolph, "The Fear of Cowardice," in *Postmodern Gandhi and Other Essays: Gandhi in the World and at Home* (Chicago: University of Chicago Press, 2006), pp. 177–98.

30. Mukherjee, *Dutt*, pp. 226–7. In support of this contention about Tod's enormous influence, she footnotes a chapter, "Tod's Rajasthan and the Bengali Imagination," in her book *Elusive Terrain: Culture and Literary Memory* (Delhi: Oxford University Press, 2008).

31. Mukherjee, *Dutt*, p. 227.

32. Mukherjee, *Dutt*, p. 227.

33. Mukherjee, *Dutt*, p. 227.

34. Mukherjee, *Dutt*, p. 228.

35. Tod, *Annals*, I, lxiii.

36. *Collected Works of Mahatma Gandhi*, vol. 18 (New Delhi: Publications Division, Government of India, 1999), p. 189.

37. *Collected Works*, 48, p. 307.

38. Nandani Chandra, *The Classic Popular Amar Chitra Katha, 1967–2007* (New Delhi: Yoda, 2008), p. 50.

39. Chandra, *Katha*, p. 185.

40. Chandra, *Katha*, pp. 55–6.

41. Chandra, *Katha*, p. 56.

42. Chandra, *Katha*, p. 56.

43. See Lloyd I. Rudolph, "The Media and Cultural Politics," *Economic and Political Weekly* 27, no. 28 (June 1992). Republished in

The Realm of Ideas: Inquiry and Theory, Vol. I of Lloyd I. Rudolph and Susanne Hoeber Rudolph, *Explaining Indian Democracy: A Fifty-Year Perspective, 1956–2006* (New Delhi, Oxford, and New York: Oxford University Press, 2008), pp. 210–29 for how the *Ramayana* series opened the way for the rise of Hindu nationalist politics.

44. "Historicals from the very first feature film, *Raja Harischandra* (1913), have always been an important genre of Indian cinema. They have mostly had Mughal and Rajput themes." Praveen Donthi, "What Ails Gowariker's Portrait of a Lady?" *Sunday Hindustan Times*, February 24, 2008.

45. A recent example is Ashutosh Gowarikar's critically acclaimed and commercially successful historical, *Jodhaa Akbar* (2008). It challenges Tod's Mewar-centric view exemplified by Rana Pratap that Rajput kings do not bend their knee to Mughal emperors or give their daughters in marriage to them. *Jodhaa Akbar* features the marriage of the great Mughal emperor, Akbar, to a Jaipur princess, Jodhaa. The historical record supports the view that Akbar married the Amber [later Jaipur] ruler Raja Bharmal's eldest daughter, although the records do not mention her name. Indeed, Akbar like his successors, Jahangir and Shahjahan, married Rajput princesses, *inter alia*, to cement their alliances with Rajput kingdoms. See Frances H. Taft, "Honor and Alliance: Reconsidering Mughal–Rajput Marriages," in *The Idea of Rajasthan: Explorations in Regional Identity*, Vol. II: *Institutions*, Karine Schomer, Joan L. Erdman, Deryck O. Lodrick, Lloyd I. Rudolph (eds.) (New Delhi, Manohar Publishers, 1994), pp. 217–41.

4 Tod's Influence on Shyamal Das's Historiography in *Vir Vinod*

James Tod's *The Annals and Antiquities of Rajasthan* (1829 and 1830) became definitive for Rajasthan and shaped Indian nationalist, imperial, and vernacular history. In this chapter we address James Tod's influence on Kaviraj Shyamal Das's historiography in the writing of *Vir Vinod* (Heroes' Delight), perhaps India's first "modern" history in Hindi.[1] By the 1880s, when Shyamal Das was writing *Vir Vinod*, Tod's *Annals* had achieved iconic status. In the process of examining the historiographical relationship between Tod and Shyamal Das, we ask in what ways and in what sense we can speak of Shyamal Das, a *charan* (bard) whose tradition was to cultivate and create bardic literature, as one of Rajasthan's—and India's—earliest "modern" historians.

James Tod's *Annals* was already in Shyamal Das's time the dominant paradigm for understanding Rajasthan's history. We pay special attention to Tod's historiography because, as we read Shyamal Das's *Vir Vinod*, Tod's understanding of Mewar's history was the most important influence on how Shyamal Das wrote history. But Shyamal Das went beyond Tod and we want to explore why and how he did so.

As a more than usually self-conscious and reflexive historian, Shyamal Das himself is historically positioned. From a prominent charan lineage, he served the young Maharana, Sajjan Singh (1858–84, ruled 1874–84), as a personal secretary, taking a leading part in campaigns against the Bhils and in negotiations with them. Later, before Sajjan Singh's untimely death at 26 in 1884, he served as a senior administrator of the Mewar durbar. This included being asked by the Maharana to take charge of the moribund History Department created in 1861 by Maharana Shambu Singh.[2] Maharana Sajjan Singh reassigned charge of the History Department from Baksh Maturdas and Dhinkdy Udai Ram to Pandit Padma Nath and Shyamal Das. With the help of a team of specialists[3] that the Maharana authorized Shyamal Das to recruit and organize, he was given the task of writing a history of Mewar. Like Tod, who focused on Mewar in his *Annals* but went well beyond it to include most of the states of Rajputana, Shyamal Das went beyond his charge to write a history of Rajasthan as it was expressed in the region's kingdoms. The result was *Vir Vinod*, a massive work of 2,259 pages including invaluable documentary appendices, many of which are no longer available. Organized in two parts, it was eventually bound in four volumes.

Most readers of the history of Rajasthan are familiar with the oft-told tale of Maharana Fateh Singh's (b. 1849–d. 1930, ruled 1884–1930) alleged unhappiness with the result. Printed between 1886 and 1893—the exact timing remains uncertain—the unbound sheets were locked up and were not made officially available to the public until after Fateh Singh's death in 1930. The history was not made available for public sale until July 1947, the eve of independence and the subsequent "integration" of the princely states into the new independent nation.

A princely state historian is differently positioned than a durbar charan. Shyamal Das, be it noted, was appointed the head of a state-supported History Department with a professional staff and a large budget. This position was probably a first for Rajasthan's princely states, perhaps even for British India. Such a position was *terra incognita* in Shyamal Das's time. But a princely-state historian, like a durbar charan, is positioned not only by his official role but also by the environment in which that role is situated. Like a charan, he is located in a court society and culture[4] and, as a historian, in the historiographical traditions and legacies of his time and place.

He has to make choices not only in interpreting the role of "historian" but also among the contested perspectives found within Rajasthan's sense of itself and of its past.

Among the most powerful influences is patronage. Who provides patronage and to what ends? We see the practical result of the answer to this question in the differing fate of the project to research, write, and publish *Vir Vinod* under Maharana Sajjan Singh, ready for and receptive to change, and under Fateh Singh, distrustful of change in general and of modern British influences in particular and of the ambitions of his *sardars* (titled estate holders). Let us look a little more closely at the effect of state patronage, at what, in princely-state times, can be understood as the effect of court society and durbar culture on the intellectual and moral environment which shapes historiography. Doing so may help us to understand the circumstances that might have affected how Shyamal Das wrote history.

Different Rajputana princes positioned themselves very differently with respect to the meaning of the past and to the philosophical and cultural issues the past encompassed. We have witnessed this at the quotidian level in our work on the diary of Amar Singh, the Kanota Thakur and military officer whose 89-volume diary was written on a daily basis for the 44 years between 1898 and 1942.[5] The retrospect of the diary's early years brings into focus the court societies and durbar cultures of Jodhpur, Jaipur, and Udaipur in the time of Sir Pratap Singh, Maharaja Madho Singh, and Maharana Fateh

Singh, roughly the 40 years between 1880 and 1920. Each court represents distinctive positions with respect to tradition and reform, including relationships with the British Raj; the meaning and practice of religion; and the treatment of art and architecture. At the turn of the century, the Jodhpur and Jaipur court societies of Sir Pratap and Madho Singh, with which Amar Singh is intimately connected, and the Udaipur court of Fateh Singh present very different ways of life and world views. At Jodhpur we witness the effect of the regent, the Spartan Sir Pratap Singh, an admirer and favorite of Queen Victoria, and of Sardar Singh, the dissolute, fun-loving young Maharaja. Although their outlooks clashed on certain dimensions, the result of the contending courts at Jodhpur was an atmosphere that encouraged social mixing with British officials and foreign visitors. The fashion-seeking Sardar Singh likes parties with drinks and dancing and does not insist on strict purdah. His maharani, although concerned about privacy, goes out in an "open" carriage and likes to hunt. Architecture, epitomized by the larger-than-life Umaid Bhavan, follows British taste and design.

At Jaipur, on the other hand, Maharaja Madho Singh cultivates a climate of purity and conscious orthopraxy. Dining with foreigners is frowned upon; when Amar Singh has an interview with Madho Singh in Mussoorie in 1903, he hides the fact that he is about to have breakfast at the chic, cosmopolitan Charleville Hotel. Hunting too is frowned upon in Jaipur. Sports in general, in which the English tend to share, are discouraged. The pleasures of Sir Swinton Jacob's tennis parties where English is *de rigueur* cost Amar Singh dearly at court. Madho Singh builds a guest house for foreign visitors in the approved Indo-Saracenic style but does so outside the main compound of the City Palace where it would not contaminate the "Hindu" architecture within.[6] At Jodhpur, Sir Pratap and the then Captain Beatson form a fast friendship. In the 1880s they create and introduce modern polo in northern India. The ascetic habits and Arya Samajist morals of Sir Pratap have little in common with Madho Singh's Hindu orthodoxy, extensive *zenana*, and love of ease and pleasure.

Meanwhile, at Udaipur, Fateh Singh, like the pollution-conscious Madho Singh—only more so—avoids inter-dining and English society but loves to hunt, making large tracts of the *khalsa* (crown lands) a hunting preserve where forests are protected and *machans* (shooting boxes) abound. To deter British intervention, he reduces railroad mileage and moves the terminus outside of the Udaipur valley. In the name of preserving Mewar art from alien influences he bans foreign painters and painting, a policy that yields the distinctive Mewar miniature style featured in Andrew Topsfield's *The City Palace Museum, Udaipur: Paintings of Mewar Court Life*.[7] In the interest of preserving its physical record if not the substance of Mewar's ancient glory, he spends lakhs on restoring the magnificent, historic forts at Chitor and Kumbalgarh.

When we say that Shyamal Das was positioned in writing *Vir Vinod*, we have in mind not only medium-term contexts of the kind we have just highlighted for the Sir Pratap, Madho

Singh, and Fateh Singh eras of Jodhpur, Jaipur, and Udaipur court society and culture respectively, but also longer-term contestations in the Mughal and British eras over adaptation or resistance to the empire and the sharing of sovereignty and culture. Shyamal Das has to position himself with respect to this contest because, as a Mewar historian writing about Mewar history, he is an heir to the self-identification of Mewar as the seat of a regional kingdom's resistance to Akbar's Mughal Empire and as the bearer, in Tod's phrase, of "national liberty." When he begins *Vir Vinod* under the patronage of Maharana Sajjan Singh, he does not have to worry too much about whether or to what degree he celebrates or criticizes Mewar's political and cultural relations to the empire. The cosmopolitan Sajjan Singh is open to the winds of change and to the contest of cultures. In this respect he is like several other rulers of that period—Sir Pratap at Jodhpur, Ram Singh (1835–80) at Jaipur—and unlike several others, Fateh Singh, his successor at Udaipur, and Madho Singh at Jaipur. Shyamal Das the historian was affected by the change in the climate of opinion and policy that followed the succession from Sajjan Singh to Fateh Singh.

Court Society and Historiography

This may be a good place to say a few more words about a term we have been using in connection with how a historian's "position" affects his historiography. We take the term from Norbert Elias, whose book *The Court Society* uses the concept to analyze and explain Europe's absolute monarchies, particularly the monarch of the most exemplary and influential of them, the French king Louis XIV. Elias is a sociologist working within a version of the Weberian paradigm, a version that takes Weber's "ideal types"—what Elias calls figurations—as "real" things or objective truths. These persistent patterns enable us to escape the study of uniqueness and the particular, which, according to Elias, plagues the study of history, with each generation re-reading the evidence, even new evidence, in the light of its contemporary concerns and world view. "These figurations," Elias tells us, "are just as real as the individual people forming them. What still seems difficult to grasp today is the fact that these figurations formed by the people can have a slower rate of transformation than the individual people forming them."[8]

Elias tries to establish the concept of "court society" as similar to those concepts we often use in history and social science, such as industrial society, agrarian society, feudal society, capitalist society, which invoke mode and relations of production, culture, status or power, master variables or determinants. Here we add a dimension to Elias's structural explanation of "positioning" by speaking of "court culture", by which we mean to invoke not only world view and ideological currents but also the kinds of variations and contestations among them found in the courts of Jodhpur, Jaipur, and Udaipur during the years that Shyamal Das wrote and tried to publish *Vir Vinod*.

Shyamal Das is "positioned" and, in this sense, constrained not only by the framework of Mewar court society but also by the elements within it—the Rajput sardars who sit with the Maharana in the Mewar court, the Hindu and Jain Oswals and Mehtas, both *mutsaddi* (state servants/"bureaucrats")[9] and merchants/financiers, the Brahmins (priests) of the court and of such temples as Eklingji and Jagdish at Udaipur, "foreigners," mostly from Bengal and Kashmir, also in service to the state, and court and *thikana* (landed estate) charans who write and recite *dohas* (couplets) as well as serve the durbar. All these are components of Udaipur's court society, a society that constitutes as well as enacts who and what they are and do. Shyamal Das, as we have seen, embarks on a new role, a new position when he becomes the head of the History Department with the charge of writing a history of Mewar.

Shyamal Das is an individual, a particular person whose agency contributes to changing how persons and roles in Udaipur's court society understand themselves, to what we have called court culture. He is a charan from a long line of charans, but he is an inclusivist rather than an exclusivist charan. Exclusivist charans can be said to be the traditional or conventional version of a charan in that they serve their masters and patrons. For the most part this means celebrating and praising them, and occasionally criticizing them. The sacredness of a charan's life, like the sacredness of a Brahmin's life, attests to his special status and the respect in which his calling was held.

Shyamal Das's inclusivism distinguishes him from tradi-
tionalist charans. It has a number of dimensions. Perhaps the
most obvious is that he made *Vir Vinod* a history not only of
Mewar but also of the other kingdoms of Rajasthan. His inclusivism here has to be considered in light of the influence of
Tod who, while not, like Shyamal Das, an official court
historian, devoted more than half of his great work to kingdoms other than Mewar. But still, when Maharana Sajjan
Singh puts Shyamal Das in charge of a newly created Udaipur
state History Department, it was not at all clear—or mandated—
that he write, like Tod, a history of the kingdoms of Rajputana.

His inclusivism has more striking and novel dimensions.
He is self-conscious and reflexive about being a historian rather
than a charan, and about being a "modern" historian at that.
He becomes a member of the Calcutta-based Asiatic Society of
Bengal and of the London-based Royal Asiatic and Historical
Societies and contributes articles to their journals—journals
which in today's parlance we would call professional. The
articles—of which more later—are written by him in Hindi and
translated into English by his friend and colleague, Munshi
Ram Prasad. He exchanges articles and corresponds with
scholars in Europe, particularly England and Germany.

When Cecil Bendall, professor of Sanskrit at the University
of London and member of the Royal Asiatic Society, visited
Udaipur in 1885, Shyamal Das, he says, "lost no time in extending to me the right hand of fellowship.... I was very much sur-
prised to find in his library a very fine collection of books in all

the chief European languages, bearing on the history and topography of Rajputana."[10] Professor F. Kielhorn of Göttingen University (Germany), writing in English on the "Mount Abu Stone Inscription of Samarasimha" in *The Indian Antiquary* of December 1887, starts his interpretation by acknowledging that the inscription was obtained from "Kaviraj Shyamal Das ... [who] in 1886 ... edited it in full" in an article published in the *Journal of the Asiatic Society of Bengal*. These particulars, to which others can be added, including connections with American scholarship on India, suggest that Shyamal Das lived in a world of international scholarship whose mutual reference group was Indologists working not only in Rajasthan and India but also in Europe and America. Such scholars and professionals were concerned with the modern project of establishing objective knowledge.

Modern has many meanings. The meaning we have in mind here is the one that posits the existence of objective knowledge and the possibility of knowing it through rational investigation and discourse. The historical career of modernity begins, according to Stephen Toulmin in his *Cosmopolis: The Hidden Agenda of Modernity*,[11] in Europe in the mid-seventeenth century when the seemingly unending violence of the Thirty Years War, a war focused on contestation about religious truth, was gradually replaced after the Treaty of Westphalia in 1648 by the "neutral," "universal" discourse of modern (Newtonian) science, (Cartesian) philosophy, and the (Hobbesian) monopoly sovereignty of the modern state. At that time, modern knowledge acquired its positivist bias; there were ascertainable "facts," concrete forms of evidence, and shared paradigms and reasoning that could establish objective truths. "Objective truth" stood in contrast to, indeed opposed to, the imaginative truths of the legendary, the mythological, the poetic, and the divine forms of truth that can shape what we know and believe about history. These were the kinds of imaginative truths one finds in bardic literature and in religious texts that Shyamal Das consulted and sometimes followed.[12]

We do not want to confuse this sense of modern historiography with the postmodern historiography that is much in evidence today. Postmoderns argue that the imaginative truths of myth and legend, encompassing the divine and the poetic, constitute meaning and shape practice as much as or more than great historical forces such as the master variables of class and interest or macro-structural determinants such as feudalism and capitalism.

Shyamal Das lived in a liminal space between objective and imaginative truth. He meant to be modern, but, as a charan writing about Mewar, he also wrote history as an unself-conscious postmodern, that is, willing to credit the imaginative truths of bardic literature, the legendary and the divine. In constructing the role of the court historian and inventing a version of modern history for India, he turns to established models and texts. His framing of *Vir Vinod* starts with cosmological discourse that deals with the origin of the world and its people; geographic discourse that locates India and Rajasthan in physical space; and lineage discourse that locates the dynastic kingdoms of Rajasthan by identifying their mythological and historic ancestors. In these respects he follows the Persian chronicles, classical texts by his time,[13] and the Mughal gazetteer form as developed by Nainsi in his *khyats* (chronicles of states) and later in profusion by the British Raj.

Shyamal Das goes beyond such precedents to a kind of postmodern discourse when, for example, he attends to lineage, to who is descended from the solar and lunar races and from Ram and Adam, as an important source of meaning and legitimation. He is telling us "stories" which provide founding myths, myths that constitute peoples and give them an identity, their sense of who and what they are. We do not mean that he is self-consciously postmodern, only that some of what he writes in *Vir Vinod* foreshadows or anticipates how a postmodernist might write history. Had he been exclusively committed to the modern search for objective truth, he would have simply expelled accounts of descent from lunar and solar ancestors as mere myth, that is, superstructure or superstition that mystified without enlightening. He does not do so.

Tod's Influence on Shyamal Das's Historiography

Shyamal Das worked in the shadow of Col. James Tod. Not that he agreed with Tod on all points of fact or interpretation; he did not. But Shyamal Das worked in Tod's shadow in the sense that he accepted Tod's romantic paradigm, a paradigm that celebrated not only Rajputana's feudalism but more particularly Mewar's "heroic fight for independence." In Tod's interpretation, Mewar under Rana Pratap fought for national liberty against a great empire. He was writing the *Annals* when Byron and others were traveling to Greece, which they imagined as ancient Greece, the Attic home of Victorian England's classic civilization, to assist the people of that "seat of European civilization" to regain its national liberty from the Ottoman Turks' alien Islamic civilization. For Tod, an orientalist European, Mewar's struggle against Akbar's empire could have been imagined to be like the Greeks' struggle against the Ottoman Turks. He seems to have construed Mewar on the model of Greece in the 1820s. Doing so positioned Mewar in a preeminent place not only in Rajasthan's and India's but also in world history.

Here is how Tod concludes his chapter on Rana Pratap, Mewar's most illustrious and celebrated son:

> Thus closed the life of a Rajpoot whose memory is even now idolised by every Seesodia, and will continue to be so, till renewed oppression shall extinguish the remaining sparks of patriotic feeling. May that day never arrive! yet if such be her destiny, may it, at least, not be hastened by the arms of Britain. This prince ... oppose[d] the resources of a small principality against the then most powerful empire of the world ... [the Mughal empire under Akbar] whose armies were more numerous and far more efficient than any ever led by the Persian empire against the liberties of Greece.

Had Mewar possessed her Thucydides or her Xenophon, neither the wars of the Peloponnesus nor the retreat of the "the ten thousand" would have yielded more diversified incidents for the historic muse, than the deeds of this brilliant reign amid the many vicissitudes of Mewar.... There is not an alpine Aravalli that is not sanctified by some deed of Pratap—some brilliant victory or, oftener, more glorious defeat. Haldighat is the Thermopylae of Mewar; the field of Deweir her Marathon.[14]

How was it that Tod came to be such a keen admirer of Mewar? The answer lies we believe in Tod's involvement and identification with the Romantic Movement in Europe, particularly its manifestation in Britain. The Romantic Movement opposed the French revolution's enlightenment rationalism, the budding industrial revolution's commercialism, and utilitarianism's self-interested individualism. Its principal spokespersons were the Romantic poets Shelley, Keats, Wordsworth, Sir Walter Scott—author of historical novels often with feudal themes such as *Ivanhoe*—and Lord Byron. Byron's death in Greece in 1824 when Tod was writing the *Annals* was critical in bringing the governments of Europe round to support the Greece-intoxicated philhellene students and artists carrying on the Greek struggle for independence against Ottoman rule.

How did Tod become a Romantic thinker? There is no obvious answer, although the result is clear. He came of age with the Romantics. For this reason he could have shared their skeptical reaction to the rationalism of the eighteenth century's

Enlightenment project as well as their reaction to the Enlightenment's offspring, the French and industrial revolutions. But he was not formally educated, that is, he did not, like the Romantics, attend Eton or Harrow or Oxford or Cambridge. Instead, in 1799 at 17 he arrived in Bengal as an East India Company cadet and began a military career in India. One has to infer from the content and footnotes of his *Annals* that he educated himself in a most remarkable way. A careful study of his footnotes in relation to the arguments and interpretations of his text makes clear that his guru was Henry Hallam (1777–1859), author in 1818 of an influential, trend-setting two-volume work titled *View of the State of Europe during the Middle Ages*.[15] Hallam followed Edward Gibbon whose *Decline and Fall of the Roman Empire* (6 volumes, 1776–88) launched the periodization of history into ancient, medieval, and modern in making the term "middle ages" the centerpiece of his work. More important, he was among the first to begin to give medieval Europe's preeminent institution, feudalism, identified by Enlightenment thinkers as degraded, even barbaric, a good name.

Tod, driven out of India in 1822 by his East India Company superior Sir David Ochterloney's successful vendetta against his policies and authority in the western Rajputana states, was writing the *Annals* in the years immediately following the publication of Hallam's *Middle Ages*. Tod frequently cites with approval Hallam's book against the very authors that Hallam seems to admire, Hume, Gibbon, and Montesquieu. They, as children of Enlightenment rationalism, depict the middle ages as dark and depraved. By contrast, Hallam, despite his Enlightenment proclivities and anti-Catholic, anti-clerical perspective, takes a Burkean and Whiggish view of feudalism as a source of liberty and law. For acolytes of the Enlightenment and the new commercial age, the feudal era was the "dark ages." Its religious ethos and chivalric ethics were read as an era of superstitious and parasitic priests; of marauding knights and passionate, despotic kings; as an era of ignorance, violence, and poverty that stands in the way of the *douceur* of commerce and cool market calculations of gain and profit.

Hallam wrote in the shadow of Edward Gibbon's rationalist *Decline and Fall of the Roman Empire*. Its message, *inter alia*, was to justify and naturalize feudalism's "dark ages" image. By contrast, Hallam dimly discerns what Scott sees clearly behind a scrim that displays superstition, cruelty, and violence, the honor and heroism, the fealty and adventure that inspire sacrifice, service, and noble deeds. Hallam provides the intellectual and moral context out of which Tod constructs his notions of feudalism in Mewar and "national liberty," the great leitmotifs of his monumental and canonical work.

We can learn something about Tod's world view and literary style, about his metaphors and comparisons, by examining the Romantics' outlook and concerns that, via Hallam, link Tod to the Romantic era. Hallam's personal connection to the Romantic Movement can be discerned through his elder son, Arthur,[16] who as a youth of 22 "died suddenly" at Vienna in 1833. In Peter Clark's laconic account, Henry Hallam "returned from a constitutional to the hotel ... and found his son in an armchair dead."[17] Arthur had been taken on a European tour by his father, ostensibly to separate him from Emily Tennyson, Alfred Tennyson's sister, but perhaps to separate him from Alfred. Perhaps, as A.S. Byatt suggests in her novella, *The Conjugal Angel*, they were spiritual lovers deterred from physical intimacy by the conventions of their time.

Arthur was educated at Eton and Trinity College, Cambridge, where he became a member of a secret society, the Apostles. Founded in 1820 as a Christian social club, the Apostles' metaphysical liberal character articulated Romantic concerns and preoccupations. The "brethren" revered the English Romantic poets and German Romantic scholarship, then the epitome of Romantic consciousness. According to one member, "Coleridge and Wordsworth were our principal divinities...."[18] "The Romantic ethos of the group," Bernal tells us in *Black Athena*, "was intensified in 1833 by the death of [Arthur] Hallam, a brilliant young man loved by ... many of the brethren; his cult, symbolizing their own lost youth and beauty, was immortalized in Tennyson's *In Memoriam* and remained central to 'the Society' for the next forty years."[19]

Although Tod completed his *Annals* before Arthur Hallam's death, his treatment of the themes of youth and death seems closer to Arthur Hallam's and Alfred Tennyson's generation than to Henry Hallam's. In youth one has ideals and can live fully. To die while young can be sublime; it shows one has the courage and imagination to enact the ultimate experience. Here is an account given by Tod of a glorious youthful death:

> When Saloombra fell at the gate of the sun, the command devolved on the Putta of Kailwa. He was only sixteen.... Like the Spartan mother of old, [his mother] commanded him to put on the "saffron robe", and to die for Cheetore.... [Akbar] the conqueror of Cheetore, evinced an ... exalted sense ... of the merits of his foes, in erecting statues to the names of Jeimul and Putta at the most conspicuous entrance of his palace in Delhi; and they retained that distinction even when Bernier [a century later] was in India.[20]

Shyamal Das is positioned between the imaginative truth of Tod's Romantic construction of Mewar history and the objective truth of the professional historians and Indologists of his time. There were, in a sense, two Shyamal Dases, the Shyamal Das who wrote the Mewar sections of *Vir Vinod* and the Shyamal Das who wrote for the professional journals of his time; the Shyamal Das who, like Tod, credited the imaginative truths of bardic poetry, and the Shyamal Das who zealously pursued positive history in the pages of historical societies.

We want to illustrate each Shyamal Das with examples. The Shyamal Das of imaginative truth writes what we call docudramas about key events and persons in Mewar history. One docudrama tells how Man Singh of Amber failed to persuade Pratap Singh of Mewar to join the other Rajput kingdoms in sharing in the honors and benefits of the Mughal Empire. Man

Singh as a commander of Akbar's armies doubles the size of
Akbar's empire; Rana Pratap refuses to bow his head to the
emperor and fights for Mewar's independence. Shyamal Das
writes the script as if he knew what the protagonists said and
did. No contemporary sources are given; it is his imaginative
reconstruction of the story of the "dinner party" that did not
happen. Here is a translation[21] from *Vir Vinod* of Shyamal
Das's docudrama:

> With the idea of bringing Maharana Pratap Singh into the
> service of the emperor, Man Singh tried many pretexts and
> labors, but these efforts were fruitless, and the Maharana
> didn't listen to a single word. The Maharana, for the sake of
> Kunwar [son of a raja or nobleman] Man Singh, had prepa-
> rations made for a feast at Udaisagar talab [lake], and
> Kunwar Amar Singh, bringing Man Singh with him, reached
> the lake. When food was ready, Amar Singh, serving the
> food [*paroskari karke*] told Man Singh to eat. His [Man
> Singh's] idea was that the Maharana would eat with him,
> but the Maharana, objecting that his stomach had heavi-
> ness, that is to say indigestion, evaded [*thala*].[22]

Shyamal Das, in a footnote, explains that Rana Pratap's
excuse for not eating with Man Singh was merely a cover.
Actually, "he didn't because of contempt for the relationship to
the Mussalmans [*Musalmanon*]." Shyamal Das continues to put
words in the mouths of the two protagonists:

> Man Singh sent a message via Thakur Bhim Singh of Dodiya
> that I know the cure for this indigestion. Until now, we only

desired your welfare, but from now on we want to be vigilant [*hoshiyar*—careful; clever]. To which the Maharana replied, whoever comes with his own strength [if you come with your own strength] will have a reception [*peshwai*] at Malpura, and who comes with strength of his phupha [uncle, referring to Akbar, the husband of his father's sister] will be given a reception at whatever place opportunity offers.

Bhim Singh told these words exactly as rendered to Man Singh. There was a verbal quarrel between Bhim Singh and Man Singh in which Bhim Singh said that whenever you come by elephant, you will die by the lance or my name isn't Bhim Singh; bring your phupha quickly and come. Matters finished up in this [*rasviras*— tasteless back and forth?] manner, and everyone mounted their horses and left.[23]

Shyamal Das next tells a story, for which, again, he cites no contemporary evidence, that further elaborates on what he would like the reader to believe are Rana Pratap's perceptions and motives. He writes, "After Man Singh's meal, the Maharana had the eating things together with the silver and gold dishes, thrown in the lake. Where Kunwar Man Singh had been standing, he had the ground dug up by two elephants and had Ganga jal [water from the Ganges] sprinkled and all Rajputs bathed and changed their clothes." Thus far we infer that the docudrama's story is taken from various texts (*Amarkavya*; *Rajprashisht*) written 50 to 75 years after the events being described. Next Shyamal Das leads the reader to believe that his story of the dinner party is supported by a contemporary account, and not just any contemporary account but one by the noted Mughal historian of Akbar's court, Abul Fazl. He then proceeds by sleight of hand and *trompe l'oeil* to gain the benefit of contemporary authority even while denying its substance. Here is how he does it:

> Abul Fazl has independently written in the *Akbar Nama* that [now quoting] "Kunwar Man Singh etc etc reached Udaipur which is the Rana's watan. There the Rana received him and put on the Badshah's khilat with respect and took Man Singh to his house for hospitality, and, in uncivil manner [*naliyakti*–uneducated, uncultivated, "jungly"] made the objection [*ujarkarna*] that I don't have the opportunity just now of coming into his imperial presence." [End of quote from Abul Fazl].
>
> Here it is proved by the word "ujar" [objection] that he [Maharana] was not associated with the feast, and that he refused to go to the Badshah.

In a footnote (p. 148, note 1) Shyamal Das tries to explain away Abul Fazl's claim that Rana Pratap put on Akbar's *khilat*: "In my opinion, Kunwar Man Singh must have given the Badshah a description of putting on the khilat in order to show his own achievements or Abul Fazl wrote it in order to show the greatness of the Badshah."

We now turn to the other Shyamal Das, the Shyamal Das of the professional journals interested in objective truth. Those we have consulted are "The Mina Tribe of Jaipur, in Meywar," *Journal of the Asiatic Society of Bengal*, vol. LV, part I (1886); "Antiquities at Nagari," *Journal of the Asiatic Society of Bengal*, vol. LVI, part I (1887); "The Antiquity, Authenticity and Genuineness of the Epic Called *The Prithvi Raj Raso*, and Commonly Ascribed to Chand Bardai," *Journal of the Asiatic Society of Bengal*, vol. LV, part I (1886); and "Birthday of the Emperor Jalaluddin Muhammad Akbar," *Journal of the Asiatic Society of Bengal*, vol. LV, part I (1886).

Each of these articles offers fertile ground to show the learning and skill of argumentation of Shyamal Das the professional historian. Here we want to analyze only one example of Shyamal Das's qualities as a modern historian interested in objective truth. It is taken from his article on the *Prithvi Raj Raso*. Shyamal Das is engaged in showing that the text of this "famous Hindi epic—generally believed by scholars to be the work of Chand Bardai, the court bard of Prithvi Raj Chauhan, and describing the latter's history from his birth to his death— is not *genuine*, but was, in my humble opinion, fabricated several centuries after Chand's time, by a bard or bhat of Rajputana."[24] In challenging the *Prithvi Raj Raso*'s authenticity, Shyamal Das is challenging a text that is the foundation of Tod's construction of Rajput history and lineages. This text in Shyamal Das's time was accepted as an authentic and accurate version of a twelfth-century text. As such, it had become not only a canonical source for historical chronology and historical interpretation but also a principal source of Rajput and "Hindu" self-esteem. It celebrated Prithvi Raj Chauhan, ruler from Delhi of much of north India, who in 1193 (Shyamal Das's date) died in battle fighting against Shahabuddin Ghori.

Ghori's lieutenant, Qutb-ud-Aybak (of Qutb Minar fame), became the first of the Muslim Turkic or Afghan peoples to rule in north India from the end of the twelfth century until the decline of the Mughal empire following Aurangzeb's death in 1707.

What are Shyamal Das's objectives in challenging the authenticity of the *Prithvi Raj Raso* text? One is to correct the chronology of events and persons through the use of better evidence from more credible texts and from inscriptions. Another is to challenge the claim that the *Prithvi Raj Raso* is the foundational text for "Hindi poetry." His literary objective contributes to the methodology he uses to prove that the *Prithvi Raj Raso* text is not genuine.

In raising the question of the authenticity or genuineness of the text, Shyamal Das has entered into a methodological discourse about what is meant by authenticity and genuineness. In challenging the authenticity of this particular *Prithvi Raj Raso* text, is he denying that similar texts may have existed or that the text at issue may have been based on such texts? To ask such a question is to raise another one: Was Shyamal Das aware of how modern historians approach the process of recension whereby manuscript texts were periodically copied for purposes of preservation and to have additional copies? Copying led to "mistakes" and to additions and modifications that, inadvertently or advertently, changed a text's meaning or import. Does Shyamal Das's allegation that the text was "fabricated" mean that he did not understand that texts could be recensions and, as such, subject to continuous modification? His awareness of textual recension constitutes a kind of a test for his standing as a modern historian.[25]

The word "recension" does not appear in his article on the authenticity of the *Prithvi Raj Raso*. His word of choice is "fabrication," a word that leaves the question of whether or not it can be judged as a recension ambiguous. Here is what he says in a footnote about the standing of the manuscript and its relation to earlier manuscripts: "The reference given by the author [of the *Prithvi Raj Rasso*], being to MSS. [manuscripts] in his own possession and not accessible to the public, have been corrected in accordance with the complete list of the cantos of the *Prithviraj Rasso* given by me in Proceedings A.S.B. [Asiatic Society of Bengal] for 1872, p. 62."[26] This observation suggests that Shyamal Das was aware that various versions of the *Prithvi Raj Raso* are and have been extant.

On page 27 he concludes by saying, "I do not hold the narrative of the 'Prithvi Raj Rasso' to be totally incorrect; but it is clear enough, that the author must have based his fabrication on some wrong annals." Here he seems to be saying that fabrication means something like recension, that is, using "wrong annals" to reconstitute a text. Finally, in a footnote to the opening sentence of his article, where he says that "[t]he famous Hindi epic—[is] generally believed by scholars to be the work of Chand Bardai" he observes that "Mr. Beames supposes the 'Poem' to be the earliest work of Hindi Poetry; in the Journal of the A.S.B. [Asiatic Society of Bengal, 1873, P. I, No. 1, page

167] we find 'Chand is the earliest poet in the (Hindi) language'. He also says that it was written about 1200 A.D. [In Ant. Vol. I]."[27]

On the basis of his finding that the *Prithvi Raj Raso* text at issue was probably prepared between 1583 and 1614—of which more later—Shyamal Das concludes the footnote with the observation that "several Hindi poems written earlier than the 'Rasa' exist, e.g. the 'Ramayan' of Tulsi Das—the 'Rae Mul Rasa.'"[28] These texts of the late 16th or early 17th centuries, he seems to be saying, have a more credible claim to be original, that is, not to be recensions of early texts. It seems clear that what Shyamal Das means to challenge is the claim that the *Prithvi Raj Raso* text at issue is genuine, that is, the unrevised text of the late twelfth century that Tod had taken it to be. Perhaps it is safe to conclude that what Shyamal Das was up to was to deny this particular *Prithvi Raj Raso* text pride of place as the earliest example of Hindi poetry and to correct the damage it had done to history as objective truth in general and to Tod's account of the origins of Rajput lineages in particular.

Let us now turn to an example of how Shyamal Das argues his case for the inauthenticity of the *Prithvi Raj Raso* as a late twelfth-century text. In part V of the article, Shyamal Das takes up the question, "When and by whom was the Epic composed?" His method of argument and his ingenuity with respect to evidence in addressing this question is remarkable. He first argues that in poems composed in Rajputana before Akbar's time and that are still available, Persian words and expressions are rarely met with. The princes of Rajputana "opened intercourse with [the] Imperial Court during Akbar's time." Among the first was Raja Bhara Mal of Amber (Jaipur) who went to court in 1562. Braj Bhasha poetry was widely prevalent in his kingdom[29] but not Dingal poetry in Marwari which appeared later after "the intercourse of the poets of Marwar and Mewar with the Imperial Court commenced during the latter days of Akbar's reign." It was only in 1582 when Maharaja Udai Singh of Jodhpur "commenced living at Akbar's Court" that the intercourse with Marwar poets became more frequent and that several famous Hindi poets such as Tulsi Das, Kesav Das,[30] Sur Das, and so forth, got encouragement. One result of this intercourse was that "a greater proportion of Persian words found [their] way into the poems in Hindi produced in Rajputana."[31]

Next, Shyamal Das proceeds to count the proportion of words by language found in the *Prithvi Raj Raso*. He finds the proportion of Persian to Hindi, Marwari, and Sanskrit words to be 1:8 or 1:10. He next points out that it was only after 1583 that the people of Mewar commenced intercourse with the Imperial Durbar. The Maharana of the time, Pratap Singh, did not go there (and here we cannot resist contrasting Shyamal Das's cool scholarly tone with *Vir Vinod*'s more passionate language about Rana Pratap) "but some of his relatives, who were dissatisfied with him, did go, as for instance Shakat Singh [his brother], Jagmal and Sagar Singh, and many poets accompanied them; and many Persian words came to be introduced in the Dingal and Pingal poems of Mewari and Marwari tongues."[32] This evidence from the "language" of the text at issue shows decisively that it could not have been written before 1583: other evidence and reasoning showing that it had to be composed before 1613. Now Shyamal Das is in a position to conclude that the *Prithvi Raj Raso* was "composed at some date during the thirty years between 1583 and 1613."[33]

We have used this exercise in the historiography of the Tod–Shyamal Das relationship to illustrate how intellectual history and historical context shape how history is written. We also wanted to make the case, through showing the Shyamal Das of the professional journals, that this charan-turned-professional, this *chela* (disciple) of the romantic Tod, can arguably be regarded as one of India's first modern historians.

Notes

1.   See Nina Sharma and Indu Shekhar, *Becoming a Modern Historian in Princely India: An Intellectual History of Shyamal Das and His Vir Vinod* (London: Olympia Publishers, 2015).

2.   For an account of the Mewar History Department, see "Orchestrating the Writing of *Vir Vinod*," Chapter V in Sharma and Shekhar, *Becoming a Modern Historian*.

3.   For the particulars of recruiting and organizing the team of specialists and its composition, see "Orchestrating the Writing and Printing of *Vir Vinod*".

4.   Compare Norbert Elias, *The Court Society*, revised edition (Dublin: University College Dublin Press, 2006).

5.   See Lloyd I. Rudolph and Susanne Hoeber Rudolph (with Mohan Singh Kanota), *Reversing the Gaze: Amar Singh's Diary, A Colonial Subject's Narrative of Imperial India* (New Delhi: Oxford University Press, 2000).

6.   This point is elaborated in Thomas Metcalf's *An Imperial Vision: Indian Architecture and Britain's Raj* (Berkeley: University of California Press, 1989).

7.   Andrew Topsfield, *The City Palace Museum Udaipur: Paintings of Mewar Court Life* (Ahmedabad: Mapin Publishing Pvt. Ltd., 1990). Photographs by Pankaj Shah.

8.   Elias, *The Court Society*, p. 14. Elias here is positioning himself in what today we would call the agency structure debate. He seems to neglect how "individual people" and agents are the determinant of the "slower rate of transformation" that characterizes figurations or structures.

9.   See Lloyd I. Rudolph and Susanne Hoeber Rudolph, "Bureaucratic Lineages in Princely India: Elite Formation and Conflict in a Patrimonial System," and "Oligopolistic Competition among State Elites in Princely India," in *Essays on Rajputana* (New Delhi: Concept Publishing Company, 1984).

10.   Cecil Bendall, *A Journey of Literary and Archeological Research on Nepal and Northern India during the Winter of 1884–85* (Cambridge: Cambridge University Press, 1886), p. 31. Bendall praises Shyamal Das's knowledge and writing on archeological subjects and speaks highly of the research done for his forthcoming work on the history of Mewar.

11.   Stephen Toulmin, *Cosmopolis: The Hidden Agenda of Modernity* (Chicago: University of Chicago Press, 1990).

12.   For a discussion on Tod's epistemological position on bardic and sastric literature, see Chapter 3 in this volume, "Tod and Vernacular History."

13.   See Peter Hardy, *Historians of Medieval India: Studies in Indo-Muslim Historical Writing* (London: Luzac, 1960).

14.   James Tod, *The Annals and Antiquities of Rajasthan*, Vol. I (London: Routledge and Kegan Paul, 1950), p. 278.

15.   For Hallam's career as a historian, see Peter Clark, *Henry Hallam* (Boston, MA: Twayne Publishers, 1982). Much of our interpretation of Hallam the historian draws on Clark's work.

16.   For the work of Arthur Hallam the poet, see T.H. Vail Motter (ed.), *The Writings of Arthur H. Hallam* (London: Oxford University Press, 1943). For aspects of his life see Jack Kolb (ed.), *The Letters of Arthur Hallam* (Columbus, Ohio State University Press, 1981), and Martin Blockside, *A Life Lived Quickly: Tennyson's Friend Arthur Hallam and His Legend* (Eastbourne: Sussex Academic Press, 2011). According to Frances Brookfield, *The Cambridge Apostles* (London: Sir I.Pitman and Sons, 1906), as reported in Peter Clark, *Henry Hallam*, p. 19. Arthur's memory was revered by such acquaintances as William Ewart Gladstone, William Makepeace Thackeray, and Richard Chenevix Trench.

17.   Peter Clark, *Henry Hallam* (Boston, MA: Twayne Publishers, 1982), p. 19.

18.   As quoted in Martin Bernal, *Black Athena: The Afroasiatic Roots of Classical Civilization, Vol. I: The Fabrication of Ancient Greece 1785–1985* (New Brunswick, NJ: Rutgers University Press, 1987), p. 247.

19. Bernal, *Black Athena*, p. 321. Tennyson's attachment to Arthur Hallam helps to explain why Tennyson, England's future Poet Laureate, dedicated the extraordinarily long and romantic *In Memoriam* to his memory.

20. Tod, *Annals*, Vol. I, pp. 262–3. Tod cites Bernier's "Letter written in Delhi, 1st July 1663, from edition printed in London in 1684," in the author's possession. For details of Bernier's account, see Tod's footnote 4 on page 262. Tod tells us there that the impression on Bernier a century after the event was not as powerful as the charm he felt as he placed flowers on the cenotaph that marks the fall of the son of Chonda and the mansion of Putta. "Every foot of ground," he says, "is hallowed by ancient recollections."

21. We are grateful to Indu Shekhar for assisting us with this translation.

22. Shyamal Das, *Vir Vinod* (Delhi: Motilal Banarasidass, 1986).

23. Das, *Vir Vinod*.

24. Shyamal Das, "The Antiquity, Authenticity and Genuineness of the Epic Called *The Prithvi Raj Raso*," *Journal of the Asiatic Society of Bengal*, vol. LV, part I (1886), p. 5.

25. For two studies of recension, including the revision of written texts and putting oral texts of Hindi poetry in written form, see Kenneth E. Bryant, "Sagar and Mahasagar: Computer Aids to Navigation in Rajasthan's Sea of Hindi Manuscripts," and W.M. Callewaert, "Critical Editions: A Waste of Time?" in *Pathways to Literature, Art and Archaeology: Pt. Gopal Narayan Bahura Felicitation Volume*, Chandramani Singh and Neelima Vashishta (eds.)(Jaipur: Publication Scheme, 1991), Vol. I, pp. 114–32 and 133–9.

26. Das, "The Antiquity, Authenticity and Genuineness of the Epic Called *The Prithvi Raj Raso*."

27. Das, "The Antiquity, Authenticity and Genuineness of the Epic Called *The Prithvi Raj Raso*."

28. Das, "The Antiquity, Authenticity and Genuineness of the Epic Called *The Prithvi Raj Raso*."

29. See Alison Busch, "Toward New Intellectual Formations of the Hindi Past," in her *Poetry of Kings: Classical Hindi Literature of Mughal India* (New York: Oxford University Press, 2011), pp. 20–2.

30. "Keshavdas of Orcha," Chapter I in Busch, *Poetry of Kings*, pp. 23–64.

31. Das, "The Antiquity, Authenticity and Genuineness of the Epic Called *The Prithvi Raj Raso*," pp. 23–4.

32. Das, "The Antiquity, Authenticity and Genuineness of the Epic Called *The Prithvi Raj Raso*," p. 24.

33. Das, "The Antiquity, Authenticity and Genuineness of the Epic Called *The Prithvi Raj Raso*," p. 24.

5 Representing/ Re-presenting[1] Rana Pratap

Introduction to Kesri Singh's Maharana Pratap: The Hero of Haldighati[2]

Introductory Note: How the Rudolphs Met Kesri Singh[3]

[When we first came to India and Rajasthan in 1956] Rajasthan's Rajput jagirdars and lesser gentry were next on the agenda of a state and national government committed to land reform and to dismantling India's old regime. When we moved into Bissau House in

Jaipur its master, Thakur Raghubir Singh, was a major figure in Rajasthan society and political life and his city home an important gathering place for the old regime's lords whose large estates were being "resumed" with compensation by the recently elected Rajasthan government. A steady stream of anxious rajas and raos and Thakur sahibs along with a sprinkling of princes were frequent guests. Over drinks and dinner that lasted past midnight they teased and ragged each other by reciting dohas (couplets) that impugned an ancestor's courage or honor, and discussed strategy and tactics. As houseguests of the Thakur sahib we sat in on their discussions of how to adapt to land reform and democracy.

Colonel Kesri Singh (1892–1980) was a frequent visitor at Bissau House. A younger brother of Amar Singh, Thakur of Kanota, he was known for his wit and storytelling. Kesri Singh was more bemused than anxious [about the land reform issue]. Unlike Amar Singh, who as the eldest son eventually inherited the Kanota title and estate, Kesri Singh was a chota bhai (younger brother) who had to live by his wits. Like many younger sons of Rajput noble houses, he had spent many years in princely state service—in Gwalior, Jaipur and Kashmir—where ability and charm helped make a man's fortune. In the late 1930s, as guardian of the children of the maharaja of Jaipur, he had lived for a time near Badminton, the duke of Beaufort's estate, and the Badminton school where "Mickey" and "Bubbles," the two eldest children of the maharaja, Man Singh, were being educated.

We found the stylishly eccentric Kesri Singh affable and charming. He affected a Loden cape and flourished an ivory cigarette *holder. As a student in Mayo College he had designed a Kanota coat of arms and referred to himself as Kesri Singh de Kanota. "Kesargarh" (Tiger Mansion), which he built for himself near the walled city, was a confection of a castle; his chauffeur-driven car had a springing tiger painted on each side. Known as a great shikari (hunter), author, raconteur and conversationalist, he could be counted on to keep royalty amused, as when Queen Elizabeth and Prince Philip visited Jaipur in 1961. Being a younger son gave him a certain perspective on his noble peers.... Having served in three states, including a spell as inspector general of Jaipur state's police, Kesri Singh knew a lot about the government and politics of princely states.*

* * *

Kesri Singh's three essays and appended notices[4] offer a creative neo-traditional interpretation of the history and historiography of Rana Pratap and the battle of Haldighati. We say historiography as well as history because how one reads the history of Rajasthan, particularly its history in Mughal times, turns on the framework used to interpret the events and motives associated with Rana Pratap at Haldighati.

The volume includes three essays. The first, "The Story of the Battle of Haldighati (A Tale Retold for the 400th Anniversary of the Battle in 1976)," is in the spirit of what we would call imaginative truth. The second, "An Essay Discussing Some of the Controversies Concerning the Battle of Haldighati," is in the spirit of positive truth. And the third,

"The Maharana and the Muse," a sample of Dingal poems on Pratap in translation, which presents an epical Pratap in the making, the poet's construction of Pratap's personality and his struggle in defense of honor and freedom against the might of the empire.

The strength and charm of Kesri Singh's essays lie in the variety of ways he tells us about the man, Pratap, and the battle. Each essay is written in a different spirit and with different methods. The essay written on the 400th anniversary of the Battle of Haldighati is crafted in the romantic mode pioneered in Rajasthan by Colonel James Tod, whose *The Annals and Antiquities of Rajasthan*[5] remains, after 175 years, the canonical work. Tod cast a long shadow. His romanticism does not arise, as Edward Said might have put it in his *Orientalism*,[6] as a strategy of subordination. Tod is very much a product of his era; he constructs Rajasthan in general and Mewar in particular in terms drawn from the rising historical and literary paradigm of his time, Romanticism.[7] He wrote in an era when Sir Walter Scott, Lord Byron, and Percy Bysshe Shelley celebrated the Greek struggle for national liberty against the rule of the allegedly despotic and alien Ottoman Turks. Byron's death in Greece in 1824, three years after the Greek struggle for independence began, symbolized the Romantics' passionate commitment to national sovereignty and freedom, terms whose career began a generation earlier in the aftermath of the French Revolution.

Tod identified Mewar with Greece: Haldighati, he says, was Mewar's Thermopylae.[8] Tod also admired European feudalism, whose fealty, heroism, and chivalry seemed to him so different from and so much more admirable than the self-interested commercial spirit then sweeping England and the continent. Tod relied on Henry Hallam's trend-setting two-volume work first published in 1819, *View of the State of Europe during the Middle Ages*.[9] Tod tells us that Hallam's story of medieval Europe drew aside "the veil of mystery which covered the subject [of the ancient feudal system of Europe], owing to its being till then imperfectly understood."[10] For Tod, Hallam was "the enlightened historian of the Feudal System in the Middle Ages." Unlike Hume, Gibbon, and Montesquieu, upon whom Tod also drew for his comparisons between European and Mewar feudalism, Hallam depicted feudal Europe not as the "dark ages" but as an era of valor and chivalry whose "natural seeds" were implanted at Mewar well before they were in Europe.

It is Tod's Romantic provenance and historiography which lie behind much writing about Rajasthan. His cadences and vocabulary, though not his factual assertions, can be heard to echo in Kesri Singh's Haldighati essay. In it he is more interested in imaginative than objective truth about the past, in truth that inspires, that shapes a vision or a myth about the past. His essay suggests that he would agree with Tod that if "the moral effect of history depend[s] on the sympathy it excites, the annals of these states possess commanding interest. The struggle of a brave people for independence during a series of ages, sacrificing whatever was dear to them for the maintenance of the religion of their forefathers, and sturdily defending to the death, and in spite of every temptation, their rights and national liberty, forms a picture which it is difficult to contemplate without emotion."[11] Like Tod, Kesri Singh says that his Haldighati essay involves "relating a tale that really thrilled me to the core." We hear echoes of Tod's passionate admiration of Mewar in Kesri Singh's "The Story of the Battle of Haldighati" and "The Maharana and the Muse" essays.

How was it that Tod came to be such a keen admirer of Mewar? The answer lies in Tod's involvement with the Romantic Movement in Europe, particularly its manifestation in Britain. The Romantic Movement opposed the French Revolution's enlightenment rationalism, the budding industrial revolution's commercialism, and utilitarianism's self-interested individualism. Its principal spokespersons were the romantic poets Shelley, Keats, and Wordsworth, Sir Walter Scott, author of feudal romances like *Ivanhoe*, and Lord Byron, the prophet of nationalism who, seemingly, gave his life in the cause of Greek freedom.

Byron, Scott, and Shelly were Tod's contemporaries. Byron died in 1824 of fever during the Greek war for independence. A decade before the revolt broke out in 1821 Byron had called for Greek independence. Shelly tragically drowned on the eve of his departure for Greece. "Throughout Western Europe the Greek War of Independence was seen as a struggle between European youthful vigour and Asiatic [Ottoman Turk] ... decadence, corruption, and cruelty."[12] The

Turks were seen as reviving "the barbarians Genghis Khan and Tamerlane," the ancestors of the Timuric Mughal dynasty.

Tod began service with the East India Company in 1799 at the age of 17. In February 1818, the 36-year-old Tod was sent to Udaipur (Mewar) as a British representative at the Rana's Court "to superintend and maintain the newly formed relations with the Rana of Mewar." His official designation was "Political Agent to the Western Rajput States." From the beginning, Tod and the Rana bonded. During five busy and momentous years Tod made the time to gather the material and to imagine what would become a foundational work in Indian history, his *The Annals and Antiquities of Rajasthan.*

In the Bardic Dingal poetry on which Tod relied, the Mughals were frequently referred to as "Turks" or "Tartars." Tod refers to the epic battle at Haldhigati between Rana Pratap and Akbar's mighty army as India's Thermopylae. In India as in Europe, the Muslim Turk was depicted as a cruel and despotic enemy of national freedom.

How did Tod become the Romantic who constructed Rajput history through a feudal metaphor? There is no obvious answer, although the result is clear. He came of age with the Romantics and in this sense could have shared in their reaction to the French and Industrial Revolutions. But there is no record of his being formally educated—that is, he did not, like the British Romantics, attend Eton, Harrow, Oxford, or Cambridge. Instead, at 17 he arrived in Bengal as an East India Company cadet and began a military career in India. One has to infer from the content and footnotes of his *Annals* that he educated himself and in a most remarkable way.

A careful study of his footnote in relation to the arguments and interpretations of his text makes clear that his guru was Henry Hallam [1777–1859]. Tod frequently cites with approval Hallam's book against the likes of Hume, Gibbon, and Montesquieu, who depict the middle ages as dark and depraved. Hallam presents the virtues of the feudal era against the Enlightenment and Utilitarian image of an era of whose religion and priests taught superstition and ignorance, whose knights glorified violence, and whose landlords perpetuated poverty. For Enlightenment and Utilitarian authors feudal Europe was an era of evil priests, parasitic nobles, and despotic kings. For Hallam it was an era when honor, heroism, and devotion inspired great deeds by great men. Hallam provides the intellectual context out of which Tod constructs his notions of feudalism in Mewar and of its struggle for "national liberty" against a despotic empire. We hear echoes of Tod's leitmotifs in Kesri Singh's essay on Haldighati.

The essay "The Maharana and the Muse" concludes the volume. Here again, voice and mood change. Rana Pratap, Kesri Singh tells us, "has remained a perennial source of inspiration for the poets."[13] What follows is a feast of Rajasthani Dingal poetry in translation. There are few, perhaps none, as well equipped as Kesri Singh to create such translations. He is a master of Dingal and of English. His translations reflect not only his command of both languages but also his poetic imagination and fluency. It takes a poet to translate a poet.

In these pages we find the poems of Pratap's contemporaries—the much cited Rathore Prithviraj; Durso, "the premier poet of his times";[14] Malo who, on meeting Pratap, "felt [his] ... body and soul cleansed of all impurities and guilt";[15] and Sandoo Rama who, wounded while "fighting along with Pratap against the imperial army of Akbar on the field of Haldighati,"[16] recounts in verse the encounter between the Mughal warrior Bahlol Khan and the Maharana.[17] Kesri Singh concludes with some nineteenth-century poems about Rana Pratap by Swami Ganeshpuri and with his own "geet" of eight stanzas about Pratap's prowess on the field of Khamnor.[18]

The poetry, unreservedly inspirational and iconographic, is epitomized by the concluding couplet by Maithili Sharan Gupta addressed to Lord Rama which, Kesri Singh avers, "could be addressed with equal truth to Pratap, the magnificent monarch of Mewar, and 'the Helicon still of the Muse.'"[19]

It is not surprising that Kesri Singh should in effect be a modern charan. Descendant of several distinguished charan families and a Mayo College graduate in an era when English was regarded as the most consequential subject of study, he reflects in his historical and literary concerns the fruits of both legacies. His reading of Rajput history reflects too, as we have noted, Tod's hermeneutic and literary language. It does not follow that he accepts Tod's history. Indeed he corrects him on several points such as who commanded the Mughal army at Haldighati and the size of the forces involved.

Kesri Singh finds Tod's account of Rana Pratap's conduct at the battle unacceptable. Pratap, he contends, did not flee the battlefield in a manner inconsistent with the Rajput ethic. His withdrawal was strategic as well as tactical, both deliberate and planned. Rana Pratap, he argues, did not "lose" the battle, as partisans of Akbar or Raja Man Singh want to claim. But neither did he "win." As Kesri Singh so felicitously puts it in his Haldighati essay, "The field no doubt remained with Man. But for the Emperor's army no victory was ever more like defeat; for Mewar, no retreat more glorious."[20] In the eyes of votaries of national liberty, Mewar in Pratap's lifetime remained independent. And if his successors, starting with his son Rana Amar Singh, made peace with the emperor in Delhi, they did so on terms that distinguished Mewar from the other Rajput states.

The Mewar of Pratap and his successors was not the Mewar of Rana Kumbha [1419–69] or Rana Sanga [1483–1527], the hegemonic state leading the "confederacy" that dominated northern India. Mewar in the Mughal era was much diminished. After Rana Pratap's heroic resistance to Mughal hegemony, the Mewar of Pratap's successors, still honored, though diminished, reluctantly participated in the shared sovereignty of the Mughal and British empires.

Why does Mewar's history matter? Because at Haldighati, Man Singh of Amber and Pratap Singh of Mewar compete for the master narrative of early modern Indian history. Pratap's struggle symbolized, in the surrogate history that Indian nationalists constructed at the turn of the century, the heroism of the freedom struggle against the despotic power of empire.

But there are other possible constructions. Man Singh of Amber was all that Pratap refused to be, commander of conquering Mughal armies, governor of Mughal provinces, an honored figure at the Mughal court who was related by marriage to Akbar,[21] courted by an Emperor who was solicitous to command his talents and preserve his loyalty. Man Singh stood in the service of a different vision of Indian state formation, one in which regional kingdoms recognized the suzerainty of a larger subcontinental polity, and in which culture was, to use a current phrase, composite. Pratap was not only the emblem of independence. He was also the emblem of the regional kingdom refusing larger subcontinental governance, and of resistance to composite culture.

Because history provides the metaphors in terms of which men and women lead their current lives, Haldighati and its symbolism will continue to attract the poet and the historian, and listeners to Kesri Singh's muse.

Notes

1. Re-presenting: presenting again, afresh.
2. Kesri Singh, *Maharana Pratap: The Hero of Haldighati* (Jodhpur: Books Treasure, 1976; revised edition 2010).

150   ROMANTICISM'S CHILD

3.   From Lloyd I. Rudolph and Susanne Hoeber Rudolph, *Reversing the Gaze: Amar Singh's Diary, A Colonial Subject's Narrative of Imperial India.* (New Delhi: Oxford University Press, 2000), pp. 22–4.

4.   The appended notices are short essays on some of the heroes who fell at Haldighati and a longer one on Raja Ram Shah, Ex-prince of Gwalior, the Tomar Rajput whom Maharana Uday Singh made an honored chief of Mewar.

5.   Colonel James Tod, *The Annals and Antiquities of Rajasthan* (London: Routledge & Kegan Paul, Ltd., 1829, 1832).

6.   Edward W. Said, *Orientalism* (New York: Random House, Inc., 1978).

7.   See Nigel Leask, *British Romantic Writers and the East* (Cambridge: Cambridge University Press, 1993).

8.   Tod, *Annals and Antiquities of Rajasthan*, Vol. I, p. 407.

9.   An eighth edition was published in London by John Murray in 1941. For more on Hallam, see Peter Clark, *Henry Hallam* (Boston: Twayne Publishers, 1982).

10.   Tod, *Annals and Antiquities of Rajasthan*, Vol. I, p. 107.

11.   Tod, *Annals and Antiquities of Rajasthan*, Vol. I, p. xix.

12.   Martin Bernal, *Black Athena: The Afroasiatic Roots of Classical Civilization* (New Brunswick, NJ: Rutgers University Press, 1987), p. 291.

13.   Singh, *Maharana Pratap*, p. 102.

14.   Singh, *Maharana Pratap*, p. 108.

15.   Singh, *Maharana Pratap*, p. 116.

16.   Singh, *Maharana Pratap*, p. 117.

17.   Singh, *Maharana Pratap*, pp. 111–20.

18.   Singh, *Maharana Pratap*, pp. 121–3.

19.   Singh, *Maharana Pratap*, p. 101.

20. Singh, *Maharana Pratap*, p. 101.

21. Man Singh's aunt, the daughter of his grandfather, Raja Bharmal of Amber, was one of Akbar's wives and is said to be Jodha Bai for whom Akbar built a palace at Fatehpur Sikri. Man Singh's sister, daughter of Raja Bhagwan Das of Amber, was married to Akbar's son, Salim, the future Emperor Jahangir. For Rajput-Mughal marriages, see Frances Taft, "Honor and Alliance: Reconsidering Mughal-Rajput Marriages," in Karine Schomer, Joan L. Erdman, Deryck O. Lodrick, and Lloyd I. Rudolph (eds.), *The Idea of Rajasthan*, Vol. II: *Institutions* (New Delhi: Manohar/American Institute of Indian Studies, 2001), pp. 217–41.

PART II: THE PARLIAMENTARY DEBATE BETWEEN TOD AND MILL

6

Jovis, 16° die Februarii, 1832.

THE RIGHT HON. SIR JAMES MACINTOSH,
IN THE CHAIR.

———————

James Mill, Esq., called in; and Examined.

James Mill, Esq.
16 February 1832.

9.   HAVE you prepared for the Committee an outline of the territories and tributaries acquired by us in
India since 1813?—I have.

[*The Witness delivered in the same.*]

10.   How many of the chiefs and princes do you consider in the light of mere pensioners, the payment of
whose pensions are stipulated by treaties?—In this statement are included tributaries, and states in alliance,

735- -VI.   A 2

without payment on the one side or the other. You may consider all those as distinct from mere state pensioners.

11. Do you consider the first nine articles in the Statement I now show you, of our political relation, as being the case of pensioners who may be excluded from our present consideration?—Yes.

12. Have the goodness to enumerate the chief subsidiary princes and the protected states?—I have in my hand a list which, I believe, contains the answer, and which, with permission of the Committee, I shall read.

Native States, with which Subsidiary Alliances exist.

Oude.	Holkar's State.	Cochin.
Nagpore.	Mysore.	Baroda.
Hydrabad.	Travancore.	Cutch.

Native States under the Protection of the British Government, but without Subsidiary Treaties. States not under British Protection.

Siccim.
The Sikh and Hill States, on the left bank of the Sutledj.

Rajpoot States - - - - -
{
Bickaneer.
Jesselmere.
Jyepore.
Joudpore.
Oudeypore.
Kotah.
Boondee.
Serowey.
Kishengurh.
Dowleah and Pertaubgurh.
Doorapoore.
Banswarra.
}

Jaut, and other States on the right bank of the Jumma.	Bhurtpore. Ulwar, or Macherry. Kerowlee.

James Mill, Esq. 16 February 1832.

Boondela States - - - - -	Sumpthur. Jhansi. Jaloun. Oorcha, or Tehree. Dutteah. Rewah.

States in Malwa - - - - -	Bhopaul. Dhar. Dewas. Rutlaum. Silana. Nursinghur. Amjherra. &c. &c. &c.

States in Guzerat - - - - -	Pahlunpore. Rahdunpore. Rajpeepla. Loonawara. Soonth. The States in the Myhee Caunta. The Kattywar States.

States on the Malabar Coast (chiefly Mahratta).	Sattarah. Sawunt Warree. Colapore. Colabba.

Burmese Frontier - - - - -	Cachar. Jyntia.

Scindia.

The Rajah of Dholapore, Barree and Rajakera

(formerly Rana of Gohud).

Runjeet Sing of Lahore.

The Ameers of Scind.

The Rajah of Nepaul.

VI.
POLITICAL OF
FOREIGN.

James Mill, Esq. 16
February 1832.

13. Where are the seats of the people called Seiks?—
The principal part of the territory they occupy is the
Punjaub or country within the five branches of the
Indus. Those under British protection are some small
communities on the left bank of the Sutledj.

14. They are a sort of predatory tribe, are they not?—
They consisted of various tribes, of unsettled and predatory habits, until they were combined (as those beyond
the Sutlej are now), under a chief of great power who has
consolidated them into a sort of kingdom, very likely,
however, to go to pieces when he dies. Properly speaking,
his territory may be considered as the only one in India
that is not substantially British dominion. The subsidiary
and protected states are, in truth, part of our empire.

15. The smaller states on the left bank of the Sutledj,
which we have taken under our protection, are not subject
to Runjeet Sing?—Those smaller states on the left bank of
the Sutledj solicited our protection, to prevent their being
swallowed up by Runjeet Sing. We willingly granted them
our protection to prevent that chief's coming more close
upon our frontier. He has agreed to respect our alliance,
to confine himself to the north bank of the Sutledj, and
not to meddle with those states.

16. Nepaul is the whole length of the northern frontier?—Not the whole, though the greater part. It is
bounded by Siccim on the east, and by Kemaon, ceded to
us, and some protected Seik states, in the west.

17. How would you class Scindia?—He is nominally
independent, but in truth, as dependent as any of the

allied states; for he is perfectly surrounded by our territories direct or allied, and can have no intercourse with
any state but our's.

VI.
POLITICAL OF
FOREIGN.

James Mill, Esq. 16
February 1832.

18. But he is an independent prince, with whom we
have treated, is he not?—He neither at present has
subsidiary alliance with us, nor do we include him among
the protected states; in that respect he stands alone; while
every state by which he is surrounded is bound not to
negotiate, except through us; by consequence, Scindia can
negotiate with none but us.

19. Malwa belonged to Scindia, and Holkar is in the
same condition?—We have a subsidiary alliance with
Holkar, whose territory is now reduced to an inconsider-
able extent. The simple mode of considering our position
in India, is to consider the extent actually pervaded by our
power, really and truly under our dominion; that is,
whether the subsidiary and protected princes are not
entirely nominal. The case is this, with respect to all of
them: we take the military powers of government entirely
into our own hands, allowing them to keep only a small
number of troops, to be employed in preserving internal
order. Now if it is considered what the military power
implies; that it is, in truth, the whole power, it will be seen
that what we do with those protected princes is merely to
delegate to them the powers of internal administration,
which, in such a case in their hands, are in truth the
powers of oppressing their subjects. This unfortunate
intermediate state between British governmental native,
is filled up with nothing but abomination.

735- -VI.   A4

20. Does this description apply to Nepaul and Ava?– Nepaul and Ava are to be classed with foreign states really out of India, with which we have only occasional intercourse; and with such our relations are merely of a commercial nature. We have agreements of this kind with several of the ruling people in the Persian Gulf, and of the maritime states to the eastward, between India and China. In fact we have hardly any political relations that deserve attention out of India. We maintain indeed a resident at the court of Persia, but with more of reference to European than Indian politics.

21. You have a resident independent of any envoy immediately from this country?–The envoy we maintain at Persia is accredited from the Bengal government. Instructions, which do not originate with the Bengal government, are commonly transmitted to the Bengal government, and forwarded to the envoy, who is put in communication with the King's minister at Constantinople and at St. Petersburgh.

22. He does not communicate with the supreme government at Calcutta?–Yes, directly.

23. And directly here?–When he thinks the emergency requires it; and then he corresponds with the secret committee.

24. Do despatches always go by the way of India?–That is the general rule; but there are exceptions when expedition is considered of importance.

25. Have the French and Dutch foreign possessions in India, or anything but factories?–Nothing deserving the

name of territory. Some small places were restored to the French at the general pacification. Pondicherry is something of a mercantile station, and they have Mahé on the Malabar coast, and some other places. The Dutch have nothing on the Indian continent.

VI.
POLITICAL OF
FOREIGN.

James Mill, Esq. 16 February 1832.

26. Have not the Swedes some?—The Swedes never had any. Serampore belongs to the Danes near Calcutta, and has been distinguished as a missionary station, most meritoriously employed in promoting the education and instruction of the natives; they have also Balasore, and they have Tranquebar, in the Madras territory.

27. Is there a French factory at Chandernagore still?— There is.

28. Singapoor is nothing but a factory of our's, is it?—It is an island conveniently situated for an emporium, a depôt of merchandize in transit; and is of importance in no other light.

29. Is it fortified?—I believe not, nor should I think it required.

30. Is it valuable as a naval station?— It is valuable as a port for merchantmen, and I believe for that only.

31. To supply the loss of Batavia or the Dutch settlements?—Batavia was not considered an important possession for us; this was reckoned a more convenient station, as in the route of all ships to the eastward.

32. Has it turned out as good and as useful as was expected?—It has answered the purposes expected from it. The quantity of traffic has not been so great as entered into certain sanguine expectations; but all the traffic the

state of the countries yields has found accommodation there, I believe sufficient.

33. You think we should not be much better off if we had Batavia?—It would probably have cost us more than it is worth.

34. Batavia would have been a Government possession, and Singapoor belongs to the Company?—Singapoor belongs to the Company.

35. Is the defence, in your opinion, of our dominions more easy from having the whole of India, not a part merely?—Greatly so. It is not easy to find a great empire with so small a frontier to defend as India, when you possess the whole; as in three parts it is bounded by the sea, and in the other by mountains, which can only be passed at a few places, or through a desert scarcely passable at all. The best of these passes, by Attock through the mountains of Cambool, we might defend (such I believe is the opinion of the best judges) against all the world.

36. What is your opinion as to the effect of the subsidiary system upon the well being of the inhabitants of the countries to which it relates?—With respect to its effect on the people of the country, my opinion is very unfavourable. The substance of the engagement we make with these princes is this: we take their military protection upon ourselves, and the military power of the state into our own hands. Having taken from them the military powers of government, that is, all the power, we then say to them, We give up to you the whole of the

powers of civil government, and will not interfere with you in the exercise of them. It is well known what the consequences are. In the collection of the revenue, one main branch of the civil administration, they extort to the utmost limits of their power, not only impoverishing, but desolating the country. In regard to the other great branch of civil government the administration of justice, there is hardly any such thing. There is no regular establishment for the administration of justice in any native state of India. Whoever is vested with a portion of power, great or small, hears causes when he pleases, and when he does not please, refuses to hear. The examination of the case is commonly very summary and hasty, and liable to be erroneous, when the examiner is not (what he is generally) appealed to by something more prevailing than a sense of justice, and then the case is decided according to the motive by which he is actuated. It has been found by experience (and the same was predicted), that misgovernment under this divided rule does go to its utmost extent, far beyond its ordinary limits, even in India. And the causes cannot but be considered equal to the effect. In the ordinary state of things in India, (though under such government as that of India there was little of anything like a regular check,) the princes stood in awe of their subjects. Insurrection against oppression was the general practice of the country. The princes knew that when mismanagement and oppression went to it certain extent, there would be

VI.
POLITICAL OF
FOREIGN.

James Mill, Esq. 16
February 1832.

revolt, and that they would stand a chance of being tumbled from their throne, and a successful leader of the
insurgents put in their place. This check is, by our interference, totally taken away; for the people know that any
attempt of their's would he utterly unavailing against
our irresistible power, accordingly no such thought
occurs to them, and they submit to every degree of
oppression that befals them. I may refer to the instances
of Oude, of the Nizam's country, and that of the
Peishwah while he was in the state of a subsidiary prince.
Misgovernment went to its ultimate excess, and there
have hardly been such specimens of misgovernment as
exhibited in those countries. Complaint has been frequently made of the effect of these subsidiary alliances,
in subduing the spirit and relaxing the springs of the
government of those native princes. It appears to me
that the subsidiary alliance does not take away the spirit
of sovereignty by degrees from those princes; this is
taken from them, along with the sovereignty, at the first
step. It does not remain to be done by degrees. We begin
by taking the military power, and when we have taken
that, we have taken all. The princes exercise all the power
that is left them to exercise, as mere trustees of our's,
and unfortunately they are very bad trustees.

37. Then upon the whole, you consider that under the
subsidiary system the people are worse off than before we
interfered at all?—Yes; and I believe that is the natural tendency of such a state of things.

38. What would be a better state of things?—There are two other modes; one, that of letting them alone altogether, not meddling with them.

39. That would he reducing it to what it was before?— Yes; and there is the other mode: when we have taken really the dominion of the country, to take the government of it wholly into our hands; and instead of leaving it to be governed abominably by the old rulers, to govern it ourselves as well as we can.

40. What is your opinion of government through the means of the dewan?—Governing by the dewan is, in reality (if I correctly take the meaning of the question), assuming powers of civil government, but under infinite disadvantages. We place a resident, who really is king of the country, whatever injunctions of non- interference he may act under. As long as the prince acts in perfect subservience, and does what is agreeable to the residents, that is, to the British Government, things go on quietly; they are managed without the resident appearing much in the administration of affairs; in the detail of the government his presence does not become conspicuous, for it goes on quietly, in a manner that is agreeable to him; but when anything of a different nature happens, the moment the prince takes a course which the British Government thing wrong, then comes clashing and disturbance. The mode of preventing such collision which has been generally resorted to, has been the creating a dewan; that is, forcing the prince to appoint a prime minister of our choosing. A

VI.
POLITICAL OF
FOREIGN.

James Mill, Esq. 16 February 1832.

dewan, or prime minister, who knows he depends on the support from British power, and would be dismissed the moment that support should be withdrawn from him, takes care to conduct business in conformity with the inclinations of the British Government.

41. You consider the dewan as a less effective or more clumsy mode of absolute government?—When you appoint a dewan, you still can interfere only in a very imperfect degree for the prevention of misrule. Unless you take the collection of the revenue into your hands, and appoint your own collectors, with your own people to supervise those collectors, you may be perfectly sure the people will be plundered. In like manner, there will be no justice unless you administer it. All you can accomplish through the dewan is, to a certain degree, to prevent the prodigal expenditure of the government, improper interference with neighbours, and the violation of some of the general and broader lines of good conduct; but you cannot, without taking the government entirely into your own hands, know that he does not overcharge the people; and you know that you cannot have any security for anything like the administration of justice. All this goes on according to the usual plan in native states, and although a dewan or minister, who manages in accordance with your wishes, endeavours to prevent abuses, the means are wanting, and it is well known that they still go on.

42. Has it not been rather the disposition of the Indian government lately to restore the princes to their sway, to

leave them to themselves, than to carry the interference further, and extend it?—The instructions sent from England have been very strong against interference, and against extending our relations at all. Both the British Legislature and the East India Company have declared strongly against extending our conquests, but every now and then it has happened that those conquests were pressed on the Indian rulers by a species of necessity. All our wars cannot perhaps be, with propriety, considered wars of necessity; but most of those by which the territories we process have been obtained, and out of which our subsidiary alliances have grown, have been wars, I think, of necessity, and not of choice. For example, the wars with Tippoo and the Mahrattas. The conquests actually made by these wars, the dominion acquired and kept, we have frequently chosen not to acknowledge. There being a certain anticipation on the part of the conquering government that the avowed conquest, taking, in short, the government of the acquired territory, simply and frankly, as we took all the military power into our hands, would raise a storm of indignation in England where, so long as we only made the conquest, but took care to call it by the wrong name, all would be very well received,—the expedient of subsidiary and protective alliances was resorted to. The misfortune is, that to elude this species of prejudice in England, we were obliged to incur all the evil of the most perfect misgovernment in those states in the mean time.

VI.
POLITICAL OF
FOREIGN.

James Mill, Esq. 16
February 1832.

VI.
POLITICAL OF
FOREIGN.

James Mill, Esq. 16
February 1832.

43. Then the spirit of those instructions is diametrically opposed to your opinion of what would be the best thing for the happiness of the people?—In my opinion the best thing for the happiness of the people is, that our government should be nominally, as well as really, extended over those territories; that our own modes of governing should be adopted, and our own people put in the charge of the government.

44. That would lead to the deposing of the native princes, would it not?—It would lead to the making then all Rajahs of Tanjore, with palaces to live in, and liberal pensions, both for comfort and dignity, assigned them.

45. Do you imagine that the influence of the resident is never applied to alleviate the sufferings of the people?— It is always applied; sometimes more, sometimes less directly, but under infinite disadvantages. He has no instruments in the provinces to let him know what is going on. What he hears is incidentally; he may know that the country is oppressed, not prospering; that it is impossible it should prosper, and yet find it wholly impossible to use any effectual means to prevent the mischief. Such has been found to be the case in a most remarkable degree both in the Vizīr's and Nizam's territories; and matters were still worse under the Peishwa, so long as territory was left to him.

46. In those cases, where there is no special clause, as in some cases, for larger intervention with the internal affairs of the country, the only plausible ground on which

the resident could put his interference to protect the people from oppression, would be, that the oppression might endanger the peace of the country and the produce of the revenues which paid our subsidy, and might render our protection more difficult to be afforded; do you not think so? Yes, and even on that ground, the resident is always restrained by his instructions not to interfere but on occasions of the greatest urgency. Upon certain occasions we have considered ourselves bound by some of our treaties to interfere, in order to coerce refractory subjects.

VI.
POLITICAL OF FOREIGN.

James Mill, Esq. 16 February 1832.

47. That emergency might chiefly consist in the way in which the oppression of subjects of a particular state might endanger the security of government, and increase the burden upon us in consequence of our alliance?—In the case of subjects, unless the resistance to exaction took the shape of a regular force, so as to threaten seriously the efficiency, if not the existence of the government, the resident would not think himself entitled to interfere further than by his advice.

48. Do you imagine the people themselves had rather be under the immediate dominion of the Company than that of their own native princes, circumstanced as those princes are?—The question admits of two answers; one, as regards the class of people who have held the powers of government, or might hope again to hold them under native princes. They are of course averse to our rule. The mass of the people, I believe, care very little by what sort of persons they are governed. They hardly think at all

VI.
POLITICAL OF
FOREIGN.

James Mill, Esq. 16
February 1832.

about the matter. They think of the present pressure and of relief from that pressure; but if they find themselves at peace in their dwellings and their fields, and are not burthened by too heavy an annual exaction, they are equally contented whether their comfort is under rulers with turbans or hats.

49. Then it brings itself to this: whether the immediate government of the Company is better than the intermediate or virtual government?—Yes; I consider the only other choice, that of leaving the entire dominion to the princes themselves, as wholly out of the question. I conceive that territories not only surrounding our own, but actually mixed with them, given up to princes whose great and almost sole object of ambition is to maintain a great rabble of irregular troops, more than they are able to pay; who are therefore perpetually hurried on to enterprizes of plunder, for the gratification of their predatory bands, are inconsistent with relations of amity. It would be impossible for us ever to feel in security against neighbours of this description, quarrelling with and plundering one another, and perpetually tempted, by the riches of our peaceful dominions, to turn their ravages upon them, without incurring such an expense for standing defence as would be equivalent to that of a perpetual war. The most obvious policy would call upon us to make war on those states and subdue them; which, to any power so far advanced beyond the native in civilization as the English, is never likely to be a matter of difficulty. Such a power,

finding its own views of order and regularity constantly broken in upon by neighbours of that description, is not only naturally, but in some sort inevitably, induced to go on conquering one state after another, until it has got the whole territory. When you have proceeded to that extent, where nature seems to have pointed out the most admirable boundary, then you should stop, and govern what is included as well possible.

VI.
POLITICAL OF
FOREIGN.

James Mill, Esq. 16
February 1832.

50. The seat of the Pindarees was on the Nerbudda?— Yes; to the south of Malwa, whence they carried their incursion; in every direction.

51. What has become of them?—They were entirely extirpated by Lord Hastings; I do not mean that every individual was slaughtered, they were entirely broken up, their leaders taken off, and they dispersed.

52. Had they any place that was their capital at all?— No; the different chiefs had forts and small territories, granted them chiefly by Scindia, where the marauders collected at a certain part of the year, and then issued out in parties of 500, 600, or 700 horsemen.

53. Have we not established our supremacy over all that it is desirable for us to obtain?—I consider that we have nothing now between us and the most desirable frontier every where, but the territory of Runjeet Sing. If we were threatened on the north-west frontier, for example, by an invasion of the Russians, we should, in self-defence, be obliged to take possession of the country to the foot of the hills, as we could not leave an

intermediate space, in which the enemy might establish themselves.

54. Is his country in the mountains?—He occupies the Punjaub, or the country within the streams of the Indus. The boundary between him and the Hill States is not very definite.

55. Does the pass through the mountains at Attock open into his dominions?—Attock is in his dominions.

56. Where is Cashmere?—It is a valley up in the mountains, north of the Punjaub, and belongs to Runjeet Sing.

57. You may then almost be considered to say, that India has been conquered and administered in spite of instructions from England?—To a considerable degree that is the truth.

58. What is the meaning of the word Circars, in the term Northern Circars?—Circar, means a government. The Northern Circars are on the eastern coast, south of Cuttack. They are five districts, which got that name, probably, from being under separate governments. They have always belonged to the Madras presidency.

59. Were they administered by the Madras presidency directly, or through the medium of the native princes?—By the Madras presidency directly; though in the case of some of the hill districts, where the people are wild and unmanageable, the owners, a sort of local chiefs, have not been much interfered with in the management of their own people.

60. Do they come under the head of protected states?—We do not consider them as states, but as subjects. The

Northern Circars were among the earliest of the Madras possessions.

VI.
POLITICAL OF
FOREIGN.

James Mill, Esq. 16
February 1832.

61. Have you anything further to add on the subject of the subsidiary and protected states?—I can only repeat my opinion, that their real condition, in respect to us, is that of subjugation; they are part of our dominion, which we manage by no means to the advantage either of the people of those states, or to our own advantage. And farther, we bear all the expenses of the government pretty nearly, while we obtain but a part of the revenues; and the native rulers, ruling as our delegates, are wasting the rest, and destroying the resource of the country.

62. In a financial point of view, then, a more competent incorporation would be profitable?—Decidedly so. Besides what I have already said, one thing is clear, that under an obligation to maintain subsidiary troops within the territories of these states, you incur an unnecessary expense. A smaller force, disposed where it might act with greatest advantage for general purposes, would be equally efficient for general protection. It is still possible that this may be an intermediate state, through which it is expedient to pass. But what is of chief importance is duly to estimate an opinion maintained by persons of high name, whose opinions deserve the greatest attention, (among others Sir John Malcolm), the opinion that we ought to endeavour to retain this intermediate state as long as it is possible. From the view which I take of the matter, my opinion cannot but be (of little weight, indeed, compared

735- -VI.   B

with that of Sir John Malcolm), that the more speedily we get out of it the better.

63. Do you imagine that the longer it continues the greater will be the difficulty in putting an end to that eventually?—No, I think that by degrees we are proceeding towards it; and one effect of it, pointed out not by those who, under the name of conservative policy, would preserve the intermediate state as long as possible, is, that in the mean time these troublesome parties, the old military families who formerly enjoyed power, and do not willingly give up the hope of it, are gradually worn out, without bringing odium upon us. They would ascribe the cause of their declension to us, if we were to take the government entirely into our own hands; but when we merely take the military power, and leave a nominal sovereignty in the hands of the old sovereigns, they are equally unemployed and exposed to this decline and gradual annihilation, but do not seem to owe their calamities to us. I believe, however, that a good deal of this supposed advantage is fanciful; for they are not so ignorant as not to know that we are the cause of all the change which has taken place.

64. Do you conceive that it will be facilitated, the assumption of the power, by its still being allowed to continue some time longer?—I think the facilitation is more with respect to English feeling and prejudice than to India. There would be very little risk, I think in putting all the subsidiary and protected powers in the state of the

Rajah of Tanjore by judicious means; but I conceive there would be a very great outcry against it in England.

VI.
POLITICAL OF
FOREIGN.

James Mill, Esq. 16
February 1832.

65. If you took the whole of the government, you would take the whole of the revenues?—Yes, and grant pensions to the chiefs.

66. You think the best policy would be always to have that object in view and that tendency?—Yes, and to accomplish it according as circumstances would allow.

67. Taking advantage of opportunities as they occur for realizing that system?—Yes, it is a result to which the nature of things is carrying us; it is inevitable; in the mean time the present state is attended with deplorable consequences; my opinion is, that it ought to be as short as you can conveniently make it.

68. During this suspense the exaction of the revenue is so much greater, and we bear the odium of it?—Yes, certainly so.

69. The means of levying the revenue is perhaps more objectionable than the amount?—Yes, because there is endless fraud and exaction by the subordinate people, who are under little or no control.

70. Do not the assignments of the revenue tend particularly to the distress of the inhabitants?—When they are not managed by our officers.

71. That is when assignments are made to individual natives for debts?—Yes, such assignments are invariably found to be a great source of oppression. When a needy government, unable to pay its creditors, gives an

735- -VI.   B

VI.
POLITICAL OF
FOREIGN.

James Mill, Esq. 16
February 1832.

assignment of the revenues of certain territories to its creditor, and permits him to collect the revenue under no restraint, he takes whatever he can get; he is not in the least interested in the welfare of the ryots, in their being enabled to cultivate their land next year or not, which the government is; he carries off the bullocks of the ryot, all his implements of industry, even his miserable furniture, and leaves him nothing.

72. Do you imagine that the native princess, who are in fact under our government attach much importance to the name and dignity of sovereign, or that they very much dislike being reduced?—Yes, they dislike it exceedingly; nothing is more ridiculous than their attachment to their mock majesty. The pageantry kept up at Delhi by the Mogul is an example. He holds his durbar every day, and gives pensions to people to come and present nuzzers, morning and evening, as if he were on a real throne.

7

Appendix, No. 13.

LETTER from Lieutenant-colonel *Tod* to
T. Hyde Villiers, Esq.

Sir,

    I HAVE the honour to acknowledge your official letter of the 9th January; and if there has been any apparent delay in this communication, it has arisen partly from the necessity of concluding my work on Rajpootana, and partly from my anxiety to form correct conclusions on the momentous subjects it embraces. The opinions I have expressed, under a full sense of the responsibility attached to their promulgation, are given without regard to any consideration but the duty which, at this crisis, requires

VI.
POLITICAL
OF
FOREIGN.

Appendix, No. 13.

Letter from
Lieut.-col. *Tod*
to
T. H. *Villiers*, Esq.

every Indian functionary to speak without reserve. If any influence preponderates, it is, perhaps, in favour of the governed; and with this object in view, if I should utter truths somewhat unpalatable, I disclaim every motive but the desire of being instrumental to good.

Though the questions propounded by the Board embrace our entire Indian possessions, I purpose to confine my observations chiefly to that portion of India with which I am most familiar; but at the same time I will not neglect the opportunity of giving an opinion on some general points where it may appear desirable. The first question belongs to this class.

> I. WHAT new acquisitions of territory have been made, and what material change or enlargement of our political relations has been effected since 1813?

IN order to the proper elucidation of this point, I submit two sketches; the one representing India in 1813, the other India in 1832; the respective colourings of which exhibit the changes made in the interval.*

From these outlines it will appear that the entire surface of India, from the Himalaya to Cape Comorin, has undergone a political metamorphosis; in which our direct

---

* I have been unable to prepare these outlines, from the same cause which has delayed the appearance of this letter; but the suggestion may easily be acted upon from the documents at the India House, and would aid to give a rapid and correct view of the question.

acquisitions, although great, are as nothing compared to the extension of our power and influence consequent to the wars of 1813 and 1817–18.

Having considered the Quere in the aggregate, I shall now restrict myself to the Central and Western portion of India; or all those regions still entitled to be styled "Independent India," between the Valley of the Indus and Boondelcund, and between the Jumna and the Nerbudda, a space comprehending 10° of latitude and 7° of longitude. Over this surface of 300,000 square miles, having a population of about 7,000,000, *i.e.* about 3,000,000 Rajpoot, the rest Mahratta, Jat and Mahomedan, and capable of yielding a revenue of 5,000,000*l.* sterling, we had neither authority nor influence in 1813. Nearly all this vast region was then under Mahratta domination. In 1832 both the spoliator and the prey, the Mahrattas and the Rajpoots, are subservient to the British Government.

Let the eye rest on the map of 1813, with its orange-coloured boundaries, denoting Mahratta dominion, and then turn to the red and blue of Britain and her allies of 1832. Of this vast region the Chumbul river has been made the great political boundary[†]; a character first applied to it by Marquess Hastings in 1817, as the basis of his policy; but, unhappily for Rajpootana, when complete

VI.
POLITICAL
OF
FOREIGN.

Appendix, No. 13.

Letter from
Lieut.-col. *Tod*
to
T H Villiers, Esq.

[†] I present a copy of my own map of Central and Western India, which will show the existing boundaries of every power in those regions.

VI.
POLITICAL
OF
FOREIGN.

Appendix, No. 13.

Letter from
Lieut.-col. *Tod*
to
T. H. *Villiers*, Esq.

success had crowned our arms against the last confederation of our enemies, and the maturing of this plan rested
solely with ourselves, it was partially abandoned, and
many rich districts, forfeited by the perfidy of Sindia
and Holcar, west of the river, were restored to these chiefs.
The districts of Ruttungurh, Kheyri, Jeerun, Neemutch,
Jawud, belonging to Méwar, and worth 10 lacs annually,
are in Sindia's hands; and Rampoora, Bhanpoora,‡
Malhargurh and Neembahaira, worth as much more, and
also appertaining to Méwar, were left in Holcar's hands,
or in those of his traitorous partisans. Who will question
that those 20 lacs of territory should rather have reverted
to a state of 1,100 years duration, than have been assigned
for the support of a mercenary soldiery, who would turn
against us on the first prospect of success?

Eastward of the Chumbul, to our frontier of
Boondelcund, Mahratta power predominates; and Sindia,
either as sovereign lord or lord paramount receiving
tribute, possesses continuous rule from the Jumna to the
Nerbudda, and westward almost to the Gulf of Cambay.
Kotah is the only Rajpoot principality east of the Chumbul
(besides the little Mahomedan state of Bhopal, and the
two small districts of Meer Khan) which intervenes to
break the unity of Mahratta sway in all this region,
embracing Central Rajwarra and Malwa.

In 1813, throughout this immense region, whether east
or west of the Chumbul, we possessed not a single foot of

‡ Part of this district lies east of the Chumbul.

land; and our sole influence was that extorted from the
fears and hatred of Sindia and Holcar, who equally desired
our annihilation; and the one joined our foes covertly, the
other openly. But the results were different: Holcar was
deprived of the power to do mischief, while Sindia rather
benefited by his treachery, from exchanges which
consolidated his dominions. Our influence over Holcar's
court is complete; his territories lying between our two
subsidiary camps at Mhow and Neemutch. To a certain
extent, though far less than with Holcar, our ascendancy at
Sindia's court is great; and so long as no enemy appears to
oppose us, we shall experience unqualified submission;
but we must not forget that we have successively driven
them from Delhi, the Punjab and the Ganges, wrested
Rajpootana from their grasp, and confined them between
the Chumbul and the Nerbudda. It would have been wise
had they only been permitted to reflect on these mortifying
facts as patéls[*] of the Dekhan, when their power of injuring
us would have been paralysed.

In 1818 we lost an opportunity, never to be regained, for
utterly destroying the baneful influence of the Mahrattas
north of the Nerbudda; and with this the power of restoring
all those ancient petty states in Central Rajwarra, which fell
a prey, one after the other, to our successes over the
Mahrattas in the wars of 1803-4; between which period
and 1818, Sheopoor, Kheechiwarra, Omutwarra, Chanderi,

VI.
POLITICAL
OF
FOREIGN.

Appendix, No. 13.

Letter from
Lieut.-col. *Tod*
to
T. H. *Villiers*, Esq.

---

[*] Sindia's original rank in society.

VI.
POLITICAL
OF
FOREIGN.

Appendix, No. 13.

Letter from
Lieut.-col. *Tod*
to
T. H. *Villiers*, Esq.

Gohud Gwalior and Gurra-Kotah, capable of yielding 80 lacs of revenue, fell to Sindia, and are now apportioned into fiefs for the maintenance of his mercenary hordes. If, instead of the impolitic magnanimity, so unsuited to the character of those we had to deal with, and so ill appreciated by them, when Sindia's treachery was made manifest, we had acted towards the Central as we did towards the Western States, and formed a confederation entirely at our disposal, there would have been both justice and good policy in the measure. But our leniency has left a mortal foe in the heart of a warlike and idle population, who, from mere want of employment, would join in any commotion. If a foot of land were to be left to either Holcar or Sindia, north of the Nerbudda, it should have been restricted to their zemindaries round Oojein and Indore.

Throughout all this extensive region, termed Central and Western India, over which our influence is supreme, our sole acquisition of territory is the important fortress of Ajmér and its lands, yielding about four lacs annually.

II. WHAT is the actual condition of our relations with these States?

OUR relations with all the States of Rajpootana are of a uniform character, but with shades of modification, namely, protection on our part, for the admission of our supremacy on theirs; and while we guarantee them from every species of interference in their internal administration, we claim the privilege of arbitrating their international disputes, and the control of their mutual political relations. They are, both by treaty and their own desire, politically severed from the rest of India. The modifications respect the tribute, from which some, as Bikanér, Jessulmér and Kishengurh, are altogether exempt, and which in others varies with the circumstances under which their alliance with us was effected. From Jeipoor and Méwar we enjoy a stipulated (but progressive) portion of their gross revenues; from Marwar and Kotah we receive the amount which these States paid heretofore to the Mahrattas; and in other still smaller States, as those bordering on Guzzerat†, we have negotiated a progressive ratio, making ourselves amenable to the Mahratta for the amount. The tribute received is about 16½ lacs, (of which we are accountable to Sindia for the Boondi tribute); and with the revenue derived from Ajmér the sum total is about 20 lacs of rupees annually‡. It is my decided opinion that the finances of none of these States can *ever bear* any

VI.
POLITICAL
OF
FOREIGN.

Appendix, No. 13.

Letter from
Lieut.-col. *Tod*
to
T H Villiers, Esq.

---

† Dongerpoor, Pertabgurh, Deolah, Ruttun, and other chieftainships in Malwa, and on the Guzzerat frontier.

‡ Rough estimate of Tributes:

Jeipoor	-	-	-	-	-	-	8,00,000
Méwar	-	-	-	-	-	-	4,00,000
Kotah	-	-	-	-	-	-	2,60,000
Boondi	-	-	-	-	-	-	80,000
Marwar	-	-	-	-	-	-	1,08,000
						-	16,48,000
Ajmér	-	-	-	-	-	-	4,00,000
		Total	-	-	-	-	20,48,000

VI.
POLITICAL
OF
FOREIGN.

Appendix, No. 13.

Letter from
Lieut.-col. *Tod*
to
T. H. *Villiers*, Esq.

advance on the amount now exacted, as specified in the note, and that Jeipoor and Méwar* are even too heavily taxed; for it must be distinctly understood that our negotiations for tribute were founded, not on the gross income of the respective States, nor derived from the feudal lands, but solely from the khalisa or fisc. This was a wise and judicious measure; and, indeed, any treaty which should have exacted a tribute from each individual feudatory would have led to serious and endless disputes.

Independently of these pecuniary stipulations, all the allied States are under obligations to aid us, on emergency, with the whole of their forces; and with Marwar and Bhopal the amount of contingents is fixed, in the former, at 1,500 horse, and in the latter at 600 horse, and 400 foot. It has been deemed neither necessary nor politic to call on Marwar to fulfil this part of the obligation, which was entered into when the present Rajah was under temporary insanity, and in the regency of his son, a dissipated youth. The stipulation, however, has caused much disquietude, and being a dead letter, the formal renunciation of it would afford great satisfaction. It must ever be borne in mind, that any species of service from the Rajpoots, not arising out of a sense of benefits conferred upon them, would not only be worthless, but may prove a positive evil.

---

* I just learn that the tribute of Méwar is at present *three* lacs; whether this is to be the permanent rate I know not. It should be maximum.

III. WHAT is the amount of Military Force required in each instance, whether, 1st, By express stipulation; 2d, By the ordinary effect of our obligations; 3d, As a Security against extraordinary risks?

VI.
POLITICAL
OF
FOREIGN.

Appendix, No. 13.

Letter from
Lieut.-col. *Tod*
to
T. H. Villiers, Esq.

THE treaties with the Rajpoot States differ from all our former engagements in this important point, that there is no mention of *subsidiary* alliance; and the tribute which we draw from them, though galling in a financial point of view, has none of the odium that attached to paying for force which, under the name of protection from external danger, was in fact a degrading check upon themselves.

The permanent camps established amongst the Central and Western States have been happily chosen both for military and political objects. They are three in number; viz. Nusseerabad, within a few miles of Ajmér, whose castle is garrisoned by our troops, Neemutch and Mhow. Nusseerabad is in our own territory; Neemutch, in a district of the same name, was alienated by Sindia from Méwar; and Mhow is in Holcar's territory of Indore. Thus we do not exhibit a single red coat upon the lands of our Rajpoot allies to excite a feeling at variance with the independence solemnly guaranteed to them; while the camps are not only sufficiently near each other for concentration, whenever any occasion may arise, but completely interpose between the Rajpoots and the Mahrattas, over whom they are a perpetual check. In one fortnight the capital of any power in this region could be invested

735–VI.   s

VI.
POLITICAL
OF
FOREIGN.

Appendix, No. 13.

Letter from
Lieut.-col. *Tod*
to
T. H. Villiers, Esq.

by an army of 8,000 to 10,000 men. This subject will be resumed in the reply to the 7th Quere.

IV. WHAT is the character, and what [is] the extent, of the interference exercised by us in the internal affairs of the Protected States?

1. What is the real nature of the duties that belong to Political Residents and Agents?

2. What are the effects that have resulted, and those that are to be anticipated on the interests of the protected Princes, of their people, and of our own subjects, from the relation in which they stand to us, as heretofore acted upon?

BOTH the degree and character of the interference exercised in the allied States of Rajpootana vary with the circumstances under which they individually became connected with us, from the peculiarities of their political condition prior to such alliance. It was the decided intention of the Marquess of Hastings, who framed these treaties, that one uniform system should be established and maintained in this most important point, the basis of which was a rigid non-interference, alike exacted by the Rajpoots, and desired by the protecting power, which guarantees the following article in each treaty: "*The Rajah is absolute ruler of his dominions*; and the British jurisdiction shall not be introduced therein." Two years, however, had not elapsed, after the formation of these treaties, before we discovered the difficulty of adhering to this essential pledge; and with each of them it was broken. How far

these deviations have arisen from the force of circumstances, how far from the faulty construction of the
treaties, we may endeavour to point out; I shall therefore
take up a subdivision of the 4th Quere.

VI.
POLITICAL
OF
FOREIGN.

Appendix, No. 13.

Letter from
Lieut.-col. *Tod*
to
T. H. Villiers, Esq.

Section 1. What is the real nature of the duties
that belong to Political Residents and Agents?

The duties of political residents in Rajpootana were
intended to be confined to the maintenance of friendly
intercourse between the State where he resides, and the
government he represents; that he should be at hand to
arbitrate (according to the article of the treaty) any international disputes that may arise between the prince and
his neighbours; and to enforce the prohibition of all
foreign intercourse between the Rajpoots and the rest of
India. In the early stage of our alliances, the resident
agents of Méwer and Jeipoor were called upon to mediate
between the princes and their feudatories; but in both
cases the rulers of these countries especially requested this
interference for the restoration of their affairs from
anarchy. We offered, nay pressed the same mediation on
the Jodpoor prince, who throughout firmly, and perhaps
wisely rejected our aid, but, with deep penetration, made
the offer subserve his views, using it as an instrument to
effect the expulsion of nearly all the chieftains from their
estates and the country. Here a question arose, as, in all
those feudal principalities the rights of the princes and
their vassals are co-eval, being all, in fact, members of one

735-VI.   s 2

VI.
POLITICAL
OF
FOREIGN.

Appendix, No. 13.

Letter from
Lieut.-col. *Tod*
to
T. H. *Villiers*, Esq.

great patriarchial family, whether we should only proffer auxiliary mediation to the sovereign, thus applying our own monarchical principles to a dissimilar form of government; or whether, if we interfered at all, it was not equally incumbent on us to guard the well-defined rights and privileges of the feudatories against the abuse of authority, which these engagements tend to increase. This was the origin of an interference, in which, notwithstanding the stipulation in the treaties, we at once found ourselves involved. In Méwar it was unavoidable, since the balance of authority between the prince and his feudatories had been annihilated, and the country, from being a garden, had become a wilderness; but as soon as this mediation was effected, and the necessary impulse was given to the machinery of government, the chief study of the political agent was to withdraw from interference, a task of no little difficulty where there were continual demands for it, arising out of the indolence of the ruler, the intrigues of men in office, the turbulence of the feudal interest, or undue pressure upon them, or the abundant grievances of the mercantile and cultivating classes. But in addition to these causes, with two of the most important states, Méwar and Jeipoor, we left the door open to interference by the undefined nature of our tributary exactions, which were to increase in the ratio of their reviving prosperity. It was then, but at all events it is now, in our power to close this door, which leads to the worst kind of interference in their financial and territorial arrangement; for there cannot be a shadow of independence

VI.
POLITICAL
OF
FOREIGN.

Appendix, No. 13.

Letter from
Lieut.-col. *Tod*
to
T. H. Villiers, Esq.

while such a system is tolerated, which, moreover, will not fail to generate hatred and mistrust of the protecting power.

Unless it be intended to introduce, contrary to the faith of our treaties, our *direct* rule into these states, the first and most important point is to fix the rate of tribute, and to fix it as low as possible; since the sacrifice of a lac or two, while it will be a trifle to us, will be a vast benefit to these impoverished princes, whose good-will will be proportioned to the comfort and respectability we ensure to them.

In all those states there exist the materials of government; and the cement that has held them together for a period of from 700 to 1,000 years is still undestroyed, although not perceived by ordinary observers; and it is equally our duty and our interest to foster the principle of regeneration.

> Section 2. "What are the effects that have resulted, and those that are to be anticipated on the interests of the protected Princes, of their people, and of our own subjects, from the relation in which they stand to us, as heretofore acted upon?"

The result of our relations with the princes and people of Central and Western India is a state of perfect security, and the enjoyment of individual property, which they not only never knew, but of which they have not even a traditional record. Not only is the hand of rapine checked from without, but internal exaction, if not altogether

VI.
POLITICAL
OF
FOREIGN.

Appendix, No. 13.

Letter from
Lieut.-col. *Tod*
to
T. H. *Villiers*, Esq.

withdrawn, is greatly moderated. Commerce is safe, though not unshackled; and with a more liberal and comprehensive system, there is every reason to hope that all the stable articles of export produce, as cotton, indigo, sugar, opium, salt, and metals, may be greatly augmented in quantity. The product of the salt lakes* in Rajpootana has long since found its way into our provinces, and might be rendered highly beneficial to the allies and the inhabitants of our provinces, but for our Bengal salt monopoly and our protecting duties. It is the same with opium, the cultivation of which, in consequence of our monopoly, produced an activity, both in Malwa and Lower Rajpootana, quite unexampled, though the policy of this measure was very questionable, whether in a financial or moral point of view. The history of this monopoly† will show the danger with which our alliance encircles these states, and may enable the paramount power to protect them against it according to the spirit of the treaties. It affords another of the too many instances where public faith is lost sight of in the pursuit of financial or mercantile interest.

With the exception of the district of Ajmér, we possess not a foot of land in sovereignty in all the regions under our influence; and although in the treaties we expressly abjured internal interference, hardly had a state of repose succeeded the conflict of 1817-18, when,

---

* See Annals of Marwar, vol. 2, p. 173; Annals of Rajasthan.

† See Annals of Marwar, vol. 2, p. 167; and Personal Narrative. p. 629.

discovering that the chief agricultural product of Malwa and Lower Rajpootana was opium, which had progressively improved during the last 40 years, so as to compete with the Patna monopoly in the China market, we at once interposed, invading the rights of the native speculators, in order to appropriate their profits to ourselves. But monopoly in these regions produces a combination of evils; and this procedure was at once unjust, impolitic and inquisitorial: unjust, because we assumed fiscal powers in a country where our duties were simply protective, abolishing the impost and appropriating the transit duties, and deprived the local trader of a lucrative speculation: it was impolitic, because we diverted the efforts of the agricultural classes from the more important branches of husbandry; thus in a twofold sense affecting the financial resources of our allies: it was inquisitorial, because we not only sent circulars to chiefs, calling for a statement of the cultivation of the plant, but despatched agents to the opium districts to make personal inspection and reports. To these political errors we may add the immoral tendency of the measure, which led to every species of fraud. The gambling in opium was not surpassed by that of the London Stock Exchange; it seduced into speculation individuals of all ranks, from the prince to the scavenger, instances of both having come under my personal observation.

If the condition of our alliances warranted interference in the agricultural economy of these states, we might

VI.
POLITICAL
OF
FOREIGN.

Appendix, No. 13.

Letter from
Lieut.-col. *Tod*
to
T. H. Villiers, Esq

VI.
POLITICAL
OF
FOREIGN.

Appendix, No. 13.

Letter from
Lieut.-col. *Tod*
to
T. H. Villiers, Esq.

have exercised it more judiciously by following the sump-
tuary laws already known to them, and which restrict the
culture of this pernicious weed. Our Patna monopoly
would then have maintained its proper value; we should
have benefited instead of deteriorating the rural economy
of the protected states, and checked the degeneracy so
rapidly spreading over all Northern Asia, from the abuse
of this destructive drug. Instead of this, we issued man-
dates, shutting up all the accustomed outlets, and proclaimed confiscation to all opium that was seized after
such notice, fixing our own price upon it, and sending
forth *perwanas* (warrants), inviting the growers and speculators to bring the opium to the British head-quarters.

I understand that all these regulations have undergone
modification; that the chieftains have been compensated for
the loss they sustained in being deprived of the transit duties
of the trade; but although the evil may be partially, or even
entirely removed, it is not the less necessary that a broad
statement of it should be given, in order that a fixed rule of
conduct may be adopted and rigidly adhered to, to check for
the future all interference on points so purely selfish.

I will adduce another instance of the dangers to which
commercial competition subjects our alliances, in order to
enforce the necessity of the local authorities being
instructed rigidly to respect the established rights of our
allies, and to allow no prospect of gain, immediate or
remote, to interfere with their punctual fulfilment.
Our own interests are best advanced by the prosperity of
our allies.

About 18 months after the general pacification, Messrs. Bailly and Rutherford, (under the instructions of the Governor-General of Bengal, though without any ostensible appointment,) proceeded to Rajpootana to inquire into the state of its commerce, for the purpose of learning whether further international benefits might not be negotiated. Had this been the extent of their proceedings there would have been no harm, but commercial depôts were at once formed of some of the staple articles of our trade, copper, iron, &c. under the charge of *gomashtas*, or native agents. Mr. Bailly soon returned, but Mr. Rutherford continued his tour through all the capitals of Rajwarra. It is not generally known that nearly all the commercial men of Western India are of the Jain faith, the first tenet of which is the preservation of life. Mr. R., after visiting Jeipoor and Jodpoor, and there exposing samples of his commodities, repaired to Palli, the great entrepôt of Western India; but scarcely had he disclosed his object before the true spirit of commercial jealousy was manifested in a manner which produced a correspondence of no pleasant tendency between the British agent for Jodpoor and its Prince. The native merchant said that his trade was ruined if he did not at once crush this omnipotent competitor; and, to effect this, Mr. R. was accused of having, in the very sanctum of Jainism, violated the fundamental principle of their faith, of polluting the great commercial mart, Palli, by the slaughter of goats and sheep for his own food or that of his attendants.

VI.
POLITICAL
OF
FOREIGN.
———
Appendix, No. 13.

Letter from
Lieut.-col. *Tod*
to
T. H. Villiers, Esq.

735-VI.   T

VI.
POLITICAL
OF
FOREIGN.

Appendix, No. 13.

Letter from
Lieut.-col. *Tod*
to
T. H. *Villiers*, Esq.

Mr. R. denied all cognizance of the affair, and the complainants, on a formal examination before the judgment-seat of Raja Maun at Jodpoor, failed to substantiate the charge: but whether it was proved or not is quite immaterial, the very suspicion worked a kind of excommunication, and no man durst even look upon the goods of the Christian trader. He proceeded by Oodipoor to Kotah, where, though his letters of introduction procured him a very different reception, he was viewed with no less jealousy and mistrust.

If a gentleman, travelling under the passports of the two chief political agents, not only failed in his purpose but created animosity, and even horror, what might not be expected from the unrestricted resort of European adventurers to these regions, where the blood of man might be made to answer for the blood of goats, and the British Government and its allies be embroiled by even the incautious act of an individual? The merchants of all these marts and towns possess the means of obtaining every article of our commerce without our intervention; and all attempts on our part, under the mask of friendship, to multiply their facilities, will be imputed solely to the desire of enriching, not *them*, but *ourselves*.

The mischief already inflicted by the introduction of British staples is not slight, and operates as a sufficient warning. The looms of Chandéli and Runnode, so famed for the beauty of their fabrics, are now for the first time made known to the Board only to announce their destruction, together with the more ancient and better known products of Dacca and Boorhanpoor, whose purple *sin-dones* clad the Roman senator. Even Cashmere itself, whose name is connected with an article of universal luxury, bids fair to lose this distinction, and be itself indebted to Norwich.

When the financial resources of the mother country, on a more enlightened system of commercial inter-communication, will admit of our expending, as we ought, a portion of the wealth we draw from India, for the pur-poses of its general improvement, and of our abolishing or diminishing the heavy duties at home on her staple prod-ucts and manufactures, then and then only will they give our Legislature credit for good intentions towards them. But it is said that steam, that agent of destruction to manual labour, (which long must, and perhaps always will, be the sole means by which the vast population of India can be employed advantageously to themselves), has already been introduced at two of our Presidencies, and that some of our philanthropists calculate on a monopoly of grinding all the flour. Let it be remembered, however, that the sole occupation of the helpless and aged females throughout India is the grinding of flour by hand-mills; and if we deprive them of this, we consign them to certain destruction. It may be urged that many of those evils are inseparable from the age, and the inevitable results of an ever-progressing civilization; but it is a duty to retard the introduction of these innovations of genius into India, until wealth shall be more abundantly diffused by a lighter

VI.
POLITICAL
OF
FOREIGN.
———
Appendix, No. 13.
———
Letter from
Lieut.-col. *Tod*
to
T. H. Villiers, Esq

VI.
POLITICAL
OF
FOREIGN.

Appendix, No. 13.

Letter from
Lieut.-col. *Tod*
to
T. H. *Villiers*, Esq.

rate of taxation, and a cheaper system of government, when a taste may be generated for the luxuries so cheaply supplied by this potent substitute for human labour; but till this period arrives, it would be enlarging the circle of misery, and carrying to a most mischievous excess the almost unavoidable vice of our Government, that of enriching a few ephemeral strangers by taxes drawn from India, to open wider the gates of intercourse which, without great checks and limitations, would be the certain precursor of general demoralization.

V. WHAT have been the financial effects of the Conquests, and of the changes or enlargement of our Political Relations which have been made since 1813? to be exibited under the following heads:

1. Increased or decreased Revenue or Tribute.

2. Increased or decreased charge of Civil Administration.

3. Increased or decreased appropriation of Military Force.

4. Increased or decreased risk of external or internal hostility.

AN inspection of the accounts of the revenues of Ajmér and the tributes of Rajpootana can alone furnish an answer to the first and second subdivisions of this question. The third must, in like manner, be referred to the returns from the adjutant-general's offices of the different Presidencies, which will exhibit the progressive increase in our establishments consequent on the wars of 1813 and 1818.

To the fourth subdivision of this Quere, viz. "increased or decreased risk of external or internal danger," I will endeavour to reply.

It may be asserted that danger, whether external or internal, is greatly decreased since 1813, and is now confined to India north of the Nerbudda. Not that the elements of commotion, even in the decrepid states of Hydrabad, Nagpore, Mysore, or Satara, or that the military spirit or resources of the Peishwa's feudatories are extinct, but they present no specific symptom of danger; and the prohibition of all political intercommunication being strictly enforced, their gradual dissolution is inevitable. The same may be said of Sindia's government, in which the seeds of decay have been planted; and likewise of Holcar's, now scarcely meriting the name of government. There are also his ancient subordinates, the mercenary Pathans, whose disjointed and too easily acquired estates are scattered like oases over the face of the country they have ruined. All these are materials which, to a certain degree, constitute a nucleus of danger, which is increased by an invincible hatred of us, personal and political. We have bound down the evil spirits of these regions, not by the bonds of kindness (as some vainly imagine), but by the manacles of fear. They are all, however, approaching the term of their existence, and though it may be wise to watch them, it would be impolitic to hasten their extinction.

VI.
POLITICAL
OF
FOREIGN.

Appendix, No. 13.

Letter from
Lieut.-col. *Tod*
to
T. H. Villiers, Esq.

735–VI.   T 3

VI.
POLITICAL
OF
FOREIGN.

Appendix, No. 13.

Letter from
Lieut.-col. *Tod*
to
T. H. Villiers, Esq.

To the line of the Indus, including the governments of Sinde, Bhawulpoor, and the Sikhs, our utmost vigilance must be directed; nor must we overlook the warlike mountaineers of Nepaul.

Of our relations with Sinde[*] the Board may form a correct opinion from the account of Dr. Burne's mission to that country. The slightest attention to its singular government will show that it contains the seeds of destruction, and that it would require little skill to break it into factions. The policy, however, of doing so may be questioned; it is perhaps rather desirable that it should be strong and united under one head, who will have a common interest with ourselves in repelling foreign invasion, which factions always invite.

Bhawulpoor is in too perilous a position to continue long a substantive state, and will either be absorbed by the government of Sinde or by the Sikhs. Its existence, of only four generations, sprung out of Jessulmer, which state, but for timely alliance with us, bade fair to be itself eventually annihilated. This constitutes, as far as regards us, the only political importance of Bhawulpoor.

From the Sikh power, and its extraordinary head, Runjeet Sing, we have nothing to apprehend during the term of his life. Although he has cause for dislike in the supremacy over the chieftains of his nation upon our frontier (of whom the Puttiala Raja is the chief) being

---

[*] Annals of Rajasthan, vol. 2, p. 271.

snatched by us from his grasp, he is far too cautious and prudent to risk a rupture, the effects of which must recoil upon himself. He, therefore, restricts his views to the north and west of Lahore, wisely abstaining from a closer connexion with us.

To combine the Rajpoot states in a federal union, of which the British Government constituted itself protector, had been looked upon by the wisest of our Governors-General, as a *desideratum*. Such an union was justly regarded as a consolidation of the elements of fixed government against that predatory system which had so long disorganized India; and having achieved this by a policy which secures to us not only their military resources but the control of all their political relations, (and this with the least possible degree of evil,) we have not only checked that system, but have raised a barrier of the most powerful kind against invasion*. Nothing but impolitic restraints on their rising energies can neutralize the advantages of this grand conception, of recognizing states which are the natural defenders of India, and of identifying their interests with ours. Their annals teem with this kind of warfare, and their columns of victory present durable records, not only of the will but the power to repress invasions.

Danger, both external and internal, is inseparably and permanently connected with Rajpootana; and according

VI.
POLITICAL
OF
FOREIGN.

Appendix, No. 13.

Letter from
Lieut.-col. *Tod*
to
T. H. Villiers, Esq.

---

* Annals of Rajasthan, vol. 1, p. 396; vol. 2, p. 480 & 669.

VI.
POLITICAL
OF
FOREIGN.

Appendix, No. 13.

Letter from
Lieut.-col. *Tod*
to
T. H. *Villiers*, Esq.

to the policy we pursue towards this cluster of petty sovereignties, will its amount be increased or diminished. If the *spirit* of the treaties be upheld, it is no exaggeration to say, that, with a few years of prosperity, we could oppose to any enemy upon this one only vulnerable frontier, at least 50,000 Rajpoots, headed by their respective princes, who would die in our defence. This is asserted from a thorough knowledge of their character and history. The Rajpoots want no change; they only desire the recognition and inviolability of their independence; but we must bear in mind, that mere parchment obligations are good for little in the hour of danger. It is for others to decide whether they will sap the foundation of our rule by a passive indifference to the feelings of this race; or whether, by acts of kindness, generosity, and politic forbearance, they will ensure the exertion of all their moral and physical energies in one common cause with us.

We have of late heard much of Russian invasion. The progressive advance of this colossal power in Central Asia is well known; its influence from Bokhara to Lahore; and it is against this influence that we have to guard. Its constant exercise answers all the purposes of a state of actual hostility, by its operation on our finances. A Russian invasion, however, must be a work of time; the plans of Russia must be matured in Central Asia, where she must establish her power before she can hope for successful aggression; though whether the *Dowrams* could be brought to exchange their barbarous independence for Russian despotism, may be doubted. "We are content with blood, but shall never be content with a "master[†]," holds out little hope to the autocrat that such men will become the pliant instruments of his ambition. But Russian gold, and promises of plunder, might excite a combination of hordes from this the ancient *officina gentium*, which, united with the more regular armies of the Sikh chief, and the Gorkas, might doubtless embarrass us; for if ever such a contest should take place, we must count upon the hostility of every Mahratta or mercenary Pathan, whose power may survive to this epoch; and that distant frontier would be a rallying point for every discontented individual in India.

This brings me to the consideration of the most important part of the subject, our treaties with the Rajpoots, and how far their alliances increase this external danger, or the possession of their resources may diminish it.

We have only to peruse the initial article of each treaty, which declares that, "the friends and enemies of one party shall be the friends and enemies of the other;" or, as repeated in still more distinct phraseology in the 2d article, "The British government engages to protect the principality and territory of ——;" to see the full extent of our guarantees. With Jessulmér, the most remote of our allies, these articles have been slightly modified, and we are only pledged to aid her "in the event of any serious invasion directed towards her overthrow, or other danger

VI.
POLITICAL
OF
FOREIGN.

Appendix, No. 13.

Letter from
Lieut.-col. *Tod*
to
T. H. Villiers, Esq.

[†] Mr. Elphinstone's Account of Caubul.

735–VI.   U

VI.
POLITICAL
OF
FOREIGN.

Appendix, No. 13.

Letter from
Lieut.-col. *Tod*
to
T. H. *Villiers*, Esq.

of great magnitude;" and as we stipulate that this aid will only be given when she is not accessory to the aggression, and as it is open to us to put our own construction upon the degree of danger, we may, perhaps, avoid the evils of an alliance which overtly presents no equality of advantage‡.

A clear insight into the causes of the international quarrels of the Rajpoots, as well as those with their neighbours, and a knowledge of the financial and military resources of each State, are essential to the guidance of our judgment as arbitrators, and of the principles which our functionaries should adopt towards this most important portion of our Eastern Empire; but as I have enlarged upon these points in the second volume of my work, I shall here only briefly recapitulate the chief objects to which attention should be directed.

1st. Fixing the tributes, and rendering them as light, and their realization as simple as possible.

2d. The utmost caution to avoid collision between our protective camps and the princes, their chiefs or subjects, in the protected territory.

There is a third consideration arising out of our alliance with the Rajpoots, which has never yet attracted regard. It is well known that a material portion of our native army consists of Rajpoots, but only those of the Gangetic provinces, who, under the Mogul power, had long been deprived of all their old chieftains, by which the

‡ Annals of Rajasthan, vol. 2, p. 272.

spirit of clanship was destroyed, and they consequently knew no immediate head. The events of 1818 have in some degree altered this state of things. The Rajpoot Sipahis, when quartered in Rajpootana, will become better acquainted with their origin, and renew their sympathies. Prior to 1818 the native soldier was an automaton; in 1820, he was known to give a political opinion, nay, to question the justice of measures. His reasoning was morally correct, while the duty exacted from him was cold and reluctant. Hitherto there had been no community of sentiment between the Sipahis and the upstart families of Bengal, Lucknow, Hydrabad, or the Mahrattas. How widely different the case will be, when the Rajpoot Sipahi is associated with, or called upon to act against, a race with which they claim common origin, and with whose prejudices and associations their own are knit. I will exemplify this important consideration, which, even to those who have long served with the Rajpoots, may appear incomprehensible, by a dialogue I overheard between two of my Sipahis. "The sovereignty of Delhi is ours" (lit. *mine*) said one, which was stoutly denied by his antagonist, who called the other "the usurper of his rights." On inquiry, I found the disputants were a Chohan and a Juar Rajpoot, who were thus contesting the claims of their respective tribes to paramount power in India, which had been settled seven centuries before by Shahbudin. The name of the Chohan was Kulian Sing, that of the Juar, Sri Kishen; both were afterwards promoted by Lord Hastings for one

VI.
POLITICAL
OF
FOREIGN.

Appendix, No. 13.

Letter from
Lieut.-col. *Tod*
to
T. H. Villiers, Esq.

VI.
POLITICAL
OF
FOREIGN.

Appendix, No. 13.

Letter from
Lieut.-col. *Tod*
to
T. H. Villiers, Esq.

of the most brilliant acts of gallantry that occurred during the Pindarri war.

By such anecdotes we see deeply into the moral tenure by which we hold these distant realms; and may learn better to avail ourselves of the admirable materials (if rightly used) for establishing our rule over them; for the Sipahi, more especially the Hindoo, is the most loyal, devoted and affectionate soldier in the world. It must appear perfectly anomalous in the history of government that the East India Company should possess a soldiery who feed and clothe themselves (all but their red coat) on 9*l.* of annual pay. One-third of the Bengal army thus paid is calculated to be Rajpoot, all of whom can look back to some period when their ancestry possessed sovereign power; and these are the men now brought into contact for the first time with the Rajpoot tribes, still preserving a slender portion of their ancient independence. It must be obvious that anything which tends to estrange the affections of such men is most impolitic; and, therefore, any measure of economy which reduces their comforts, and interferes with the mutual sympathy between the Sipahi and his European captain, weakens one of the strongest pillars or our empire.

VI. How far have the principles of justice and expediency been adhered to?

THIS Quere opens a wide field for observation, in which difficulties of no mean kind abound. The term *expediency* has necessarily a wider sense than that of *justice*, in all our transactions with these States; and from the anomalous condition, not only of our own power, but of the governments by which we are surrounded, justice in the abstract can scarcely be a matter of discussion.

Our acts arising out of the war of 1817-18, with regard to the brave chieftains of Kheechiwarra and Gurra-Kotah, certainly violated justice, while they could hardly be defended even on the ground of expediency. Both these states, and more especially Kheechiwarra, which had maintained itself against all the Mahomedan dynasties, and though much reduced, even against Mahratta thraldom, fell victims to our alliance with Sindia in 1818, (though this chief was convicted of treason to our power,) and what he never could effect with all his means, we accomplished for him. Although these acts did not arise out of a subsidiary alliance, it was from a state of things tantamount thereto, having contingents of Sindia under our control. Some excuse may be found in the feverish anxiety to keep this Mahratta from hostilities; but it is one of those transactions in which justice was forgotten. We hunted the remains of this valiant tribe with Sindia's contingent, headed by European officers. The ancestor of the brave Kheechie chief had rendered the British Government essential service in Goddard's hazardous march, and on other occasions of our early contests with Madhaji Sindia had served with all his troops; but, instead of reaping the same reward as the chief of Bhopal for the same act, only a nook was left to him of all his ancient patrimony.

VI.
POLITICAL
OF
FOREIGN.
Appendix, No. 13.

Letter from
Lieut.-col. *Tod*
to
T. H. Villiers, Esq.

VI.
POLITICAL
OF
FOREIGN.

Appendix, No. 13.

Letter from
Lieut.-col. *Tod*
to
T. H. Villiers, Esq.

With regard to Gurra-Kotah the exercise of our power was yet more palpably unjust. This chieftainship (in the south-west corner of Boondelcund) had fought out its independence throughout all the periods of greatest violence until 1816, when Sindia at length obtained possession of it; but, taking advantage of the general hostilities of 1817, when all India was against us, the chief redeemed his possession. When the war was over, and from a policy ever to be lamented, we not only overlooked Sindia's treachery, but consolidated his power, merely on his showing that Gurra-Kotah was his, we loaded the British army with the obloquy of reducing a brave, independent chief, for the sake of ingratiating the treacherous Mahratta.

The case of the minor chief of Amud, the ancient proprietor of Rampoora-Bhampoora, is equally hard. This is an ancient fief of Méwar, belonging to the Chonderawut tribe, a branch of the Rana's family, who had held it for centuries. Rana Juggut Sing had assigned it, as a temporary provision, to his nephew, Madhu Sing, who, through Holcar's aid, contested and obtained the throne of Jeipoor against his elder brother Esuri Sing. For this service Madhu Sing made over these districts appertaining to Méwar to Holcar, with whom they have since remained. When Madhu Sing obtained them, the rights of the Chonderawuts, the feudatories of centuries, were restricted to the subordinate fortress of Amud and some 20 villages; and as the district was chiefly inhabited by this clan, Holcar's government had been compelled to respect this remnant of their power (which a century ago yielded nine lacs annually). Shortly after the events of 1818 the subject of Amud was broached by Holcar's agent to ours, and it was described by the former as a shelter for the enemies of order. Unhappily the Rao was an infant, and, as frequently happens in more civilized countries, the possession of power caused contests and parties. It was not of course deemed expedient by Holcar's government to enter into the history of the rights of this fragment of an ancient fief; disorder must be put down, and our troops went against it. Internal animosities were stopped; the garrison and the young Rao surrendered to our authority; and Amud, the last refuge of an ancient family, which had survived Arungzéb's tyranny, was blown up by the English! This was Bhurtpore upon a smaller scale, but *here* motives could not be attributed.

In all these cases we were aiding powers whose sole aim was our destruction (which by the most insidious treachery they had recently attempted) against the indigenous princes, who, by their bravery, had dragged on a precarious, but independent existence through centuries of strife.

Again, in the case of Kotah, which must be well known to the Board as involving some nice points, we found ourselves obliged to support expediency and our guarantee against justice in the abstract; but as I have elsewhere fully detailed this case, I beg to refer to it*, as likewise to the

VI.
POLITICAL
OF
FOREIGN.

Appendix, No. 13.

Letter from
Lieut.-col. *Tod*
to
T. H. Villiers, Esq.

---

* Annals of Rajasthan, vol. 2, p. 563.

VI.
POLITICAL
OF
FOREIGN.

Appendix, No. 13.

Letter from
Lieut.-col. *Tod*
to
T. H. Villiers, Esq.

question of accession to the throne of Jeipoor[†], where we supported an interloper against the lawful claimant and the established laws of succession, which might have led to serious results but for the birth of a posthumous child.

These are the most prominent cases in which we have departed from the laws of abstract justice, partly from ignorance of their past history, partly from the misrepresentations of parties calling for our supports, or from the force of circumstances which scarcely left us free agents. There are others, but as they are adverted to in the reply to Qu. VII., it is unnecessary here to pursue the subject, I will, therefore, merely observe, that upon the degree and nature of our interference with these states, and upon a proper knowledge and estimate of the varied interests that pervade them, which can alone enable the paramount power to unite justice with expediency in its relation with them, must depend the benefits which might accrue to us from these important allies.

> VII. How far have the strength and distribution of the British Indian Army been regulated by a due attention to the changes that have occurred in our political position and relations, and to their actual condition, with reference to the forces belonging to Native States, on whose aid we could depend, or against whose hostility we have to guard?

The specific objects contained in this Quere have been efficiently attained as far as regards Central and

---

† Annals of Rajasthan, vol. 2, p. 378.

Western India, both as to the positions selected for our camps, and the numerical allotment of the troops. Two chains have been extended connecting Hindust'han with the Dekhan and with Guzzerat: and a conciliatory policy towards the Rajpoots will *in time* make them powerful and indispensable links. The more eastern chain is from Allahabad and Benares, and consists of posts through Boondelcand to Hosungabad, the passage of the Nerbudda. The western chain connects the stations on the Jumna with Ajmér, Neemutch and Mhow, to Candeish; or, by means of the petty subordinate states upon the Myhie, with Guzzerat.

To render these permanent camps independent of all auxiliary aid, as well as of each other, is of primary importance. I would therefore suggest, on the score of discipline, efficiency and economy, the entire abolition of detachments and petty posts; that our armies should be condensed into masses, able, not only to defend themselves against all contingencies, but also, without long preparatory measures, to move on any threatened point and at once crush revolt. One large central camp in Boondelcund would suffice to communicate between the camps on the Nerbudda, and Allahabad, Benares and all subordinate posts should be amalgamated with it. So likewise with the western line, where the main camps of Ajmér, Neemutch and Mhow, may be strengthened by calling in all the petty outposts west of the Jumna, viz.; Goorgong, Rewarri and Hansi (excepting Skinner's horse).

VI.
POLITICAL
OF
FOREIGN.

Appendix, No. 13.

Letter from
Lieut.-col. *Tod*
to
T. H. Villiers, Esq.

VI.
POLITICAL
OF
FOREIGN.

Appendix, No. 13.

Letter from
Lieut.-col. *Tod*
to
T. H. *Villiers*, Esq.

Both in a political and military point of view, Ajmér is the key of all our positions, and must be the point of all future operations in Northern India. It should, therefore, be made powerfully independent.

The same principle of a few grand lines, defended by masses, might be extended throughout India. It is a principle in tactics that no force should be detached which cannot sustain itself, yet have we always acted in opposition to this axiom, affording in these multiplied demonstrations of our means, proof only of our weakness. The day for detachment of five companies and six-pounders for the reduction of mud forts is gone by; and the breaking up of inferior posts, which harass the men, destroy discipline, and oppress the country people, by compelling them to provide the means required to move these detachments, should follow. The line of the Ganges indicates the base of our power. The Presidency, and one intermediate station between it and Benares; strong garrisons for Allahabad and Agra, and one station between Agra and Kurnal, (which last claims the greatest importance, and of which Lodhiana is the outpost), appear to be the principal positions in which to concentrate our armies. Agra is more eligible than Mat'hura, being in the vicinity of the chief fords of the Chumbul, and equally overawing the Játs, Meerut, (with its strong outposts of Bareilly and Almora), Futtegurh, and Lucknow, appear the fittest stations for the concentration of our forces, to provide against contingencies. It might be requisite to strengthen the posts upon the Assam frontier; but the great stations of Berhampore and Cawnpore seem no longer necessary; and the troops allotted to these, with the multiplicity of petty posts, might with advantage be transferred to Benares, Agra, Lucknow, Meerut and Kurnal. Cuttack would complete the list of stations uniting the Bengal and Coast armies.

VI.
POLITICAL
OF
FOREIGN.
Appendix, No. 13.
Letter from
Lieut.-col. *Tod*
to
T. H. Villiers, Esq.

It is true that, by this distribution, the stations would be widely apart; but with so inefficient an army for such extended defence, there is no alternative between separating and weakening, or condensing and strengthening the forces. Each station should be strong enough to fight its way from one end of India to the other. Any two of these armies might unite in three weeks; and in Upper India 30,000 men might congregate in less than a month. Our policy can never be defensive; when that day comes India is lost.

The whole history of our subsidiary alliances has practically illustrated their denationalizing influence, upon the princes and the people who have been made to purchase our protection. The principle is immutable; even if it insure not sudden annihilation, it operates with equal certainty, in a slow process of decay. Where are the States which, a quarter of a century ago, were to enjoy the perpetuity of our friendship? "*Troja fuit!*" and all these camps may therefore be regarded as active agents of evil.

It is a subject of gratulation that the position of the permanent and indispensable camps at Ajmér, Neemutch, and Mhow, connecting our Gangetic Provinces with the

VI.
POLITICAL
OF
FOREIGN.

Appendix, No. 13.

Letter from
Lieut.-col. *Tod*
to
T. H. *Villiers*, Esq.

Dekhan, while they secure the objects of our supremacy, do not remind the Rajpoots of their prostration of independence, as in past times, when placed immediately under the eyes of the protected; nor does the necessity longer exist. The Mahratta was the natural foe of our power; the Rajpoot is its natural ally. Happily for them and for us, the Rajpoots have hitherto regarded these camps only as checks upon their foes, a feeling which, with proper circumspection, we may turn to our mutual advantage; and in so doing, we shall best retard the predicted period when the *maximum* of our possessions will be the *minimum* of our power.

It was well observed by Moro Dekshut, the Mahratta minister of the last Péshwa to Major Ford, "that no native power could, from its habits, conduct itself with that strict fidelity which we seemed to demand;" a remark confirmed to me by one whose penetrating mind had studied all our acts, and whose extended life had embraced nearly the whole history of our power, from the battle of Plassy to the subjugation of the Péshwa; I mean Zalim Sing of Kotah. In reply to my assertion, shortly after the opening of our intercourse, that we repudiated all idea of aggrandizement in Rajpootana: "I have no doubt you think what you say; but the period is rapidly approaching when there will be but *one coin* current throughout India."[*]

When such are the impressions of the wisest of the natives, as well as one of the most practical of our own

---

[*] The striking of coin is an act of sovereignty in the East.

politicians (Sir T. Munro), we may say the object is already half effected. Denials and renunciations are futile, for they appeal to facts—to our position; and if the impression should become general, if no method be devised to convince them that ultimate conquest is not our object, what can we expect but the conversion of our best friends into our bitterest foes? The more we consider the subject, the more difficult appears the mode of extrication. All depends, however, as before observed, on the extent and nature of our interference.

Those who look upon the several nations of India as similar in mind as in complexion can perceive no danger in extending our interference throughout the protected states. Such men take their opinions from the resistance hitherto opposed to us by upstart Mahrattas, banditti Pindarris, or rebel viceroys, between whom and their subjects no bond of union exists; but they can form no idea of the identity of interests subsisting with the Rajpoots, of whose history they are ignorant. Others again, on the score of philanthropy, contemn as inhuman and impolitic all who advocate the withdrawal of checks over their independent administration: inhuman, inasmuch as if left to themselves they might recommence their old international warfare; and impolitic, because we should relinquish what we have acquired with difficulty. A reference to their history, which will show that they now occupy the same lands where the Mahomedans found them on their conquest of India, by proving the tenacity of Rajpoot institutions and associations, may quiet

VI.
POLITICAL
OF
FOREIGN.

Appendix, No. 13.

Letter from
Lieut.-col. *Tod*
to
T. II. Villiers, Esq.

VI.
POLITICAL
OF
FOREIGN.

Appendix, No. 13.

Letter from
Lieut.-col. *Tod*
to
T. H. *Villiers*, Esq.

the fears of the philanthropists; and with regard to the impolicy, our interference cannot for an instant be justified on this ground. The arguments so justly applied to the policy of 1805, when Lord Cornwallis and Sir George Barlow annulled the grand project of Marquess Wellesley, for uniting the fixed governments of Rajpootana in one grand federal union against the predatory states, are now no longer applicable, for the Mahrattas are politically defunct. The evils of *non-interference* may be many. We should hear of border feuds, in which a few hundreds would fall on each side; followed up, if we let them alone, by an intermarriage and pacification; we might sometimes have complaints of obstructions to commerce, requiring our interposition to obtain redress; we might even be made *directly* sensible that there existed in these States men whose occasional excesses required chastisement; but these are evils inseparable from the moral and social condition equally of the Rajpoots and all Asiatic governments, and would cease with the amelioration of that condition. But are we to destroy because we cannot at once amend? or are the necessary checks to such evils, when they *do occur*, to be compared with an interference whose very nature must create such occasions?

The only safe alternative, therefore, is a re-modelling of the alliances lessening the causes of interference, by diminishing the tributes, and providing for their realization in a manner to prevent the least chance of collision; and rendering the alliance, as far as possible, one of mutual benefit and support.

Already have the evil effects of our alliances received practical illustration, in a variety of ways, in almost every state of Rajpootana. The first effect is the abolition of all those wholesome checks which restrained the passions of their princes; for, applying our own monarchical principles, we recognise only the immediate power with whom we treated, and whom we engage to support against all enemies internal and external. Being thus freed from the fear of a re-action amongst his feudatory kinsmen, the prince may pursue the dictates of a blind revenge, assured that no neighbour prince dare give sanctuary to his victims; or, if an insatiate avarice prompt him to visit the merchant and cultivator with contributions or exorbitant taxes on their labour, the sufferers have not even emigration left as a refuge. Marwar and Jessulmér have powerfully exemplified this, our alliance having completely neutralized all the checks that avarice or tyranny had to fear from the hatred of their chiefs or subjects.* The ancient balance of power, which often ended in the deposal or death of a tyrant, we have thus completely destroyed.

It would seem, indeed, that we do not rightly comprehend the scope of our own policy; for by strange inconsistency, we turned a deaf ear to the remonstrance of the chief vassals of Marwar when expelled their estates and

VI.
POLITICAL
OF
FOREIGN.

Appendix, No. 13.

Letter from
Lieut.-col. *Tod*
to
T. H. Villiers, Esq.

---

* *Vide* Letter of expatriated Chiefs of Marwar to the British Political Agent, tracing all their sufferings to the alliance. Annals of Rajasthan, vol. 1, p. 197.

VI.
POLITICAL
OF
FOREIGN.

Appendix, No. 13.

Letter from
Lieut.-col. *Tod*
to
T. H. *Villiers*, Esq.

country by their prince; and the minister of Jessulmer was allowed to pursue the plunder of his subjects with impurity; but no sooner does the Rajah of Bikanér apply to the paramount power to put down disaffection, than the aid denied to his kindred chiefs and subjects is promised to the prince. It never occurs to us that rebellion may be justifiable; it is enough that tumult exists, and that it must be repressed. The whole history of our power shows that we have hitherto acted in ignorance of the mutual relations of the princes and their people. We might plead this ignorance *pro tanto* in mitigation of the wrongs it has produced; but this plea no longer exists; and the history of Bikanér shows us that deposal would be too slight a punishment for the tyranny of this prince to his chieftains and subjects.

It is the same with the confederation of Shékhavati, of whose history our government is profoundly ignorant. Few men in India know even the name of this singular and interesting community, which has rights well defined, and quite distinct from the parent state of Jeipoor, which has never been able entirely to subvert their independence. One of the most characteristic results of these alliances is, that it encourages indolence and injustice to appeal to us to perform what their own energies have hitherto been unequal to. Thus we may send troops into Bikanér and Shékhavati, and upon most inadequate grounds commence disputes in a country where connections are so interwoven, that the first act of hostility may ramify through the whole of Rajpootana.

The natural tendency, as before remarked, of our interference between the Rajpoot Princes and their subjects, will be to bring them all eventually under direct rule; a consequence which, either as regards these people or ourselves, is to be deprecated. Not only, I conceive, would they *not* become happier, wiser, or wealthier under our sway, but we should confine a mass of elastic discontent that might ultimately explode to our mutual ruin. In substituting for the rajas and thakoors, judges and collectors, we must go beyond the tyranny of Arungzéb. Rajpootana is studded with fortresses, each of which would prove another Bhurtpore, and furnish defenders similar to those whose indomitable spirit destroyed the Mogul power. They should not imagine that, like the Moguls, we desire to subvert either their religion or their power. Let the line of separation between the controlling agent and the Rajpoots be as broad as possible; remove whatever may appear to menace their *guaranteed* independence. By these means alone can we secure in them the barrier we require against any foreign foe. Our local governments of India, which derive half their credit at home from the strength of their treasury, may not be inclined to counsel the lessening of the tributes; but be it remembered that one lac of rupees exported by force will cost millions in the end.

VI.
POLITICAL
OF
FOREIGN.

Appendix, No. 13.

Letter from
Lieut.-col. *Tod*
to
T. H. Villiers, Esq.

VI.
POLITICAL
OF
FOREIGN.

Appendix, No. 13.

Letter from
Lieut.-col. *Tod*
to
T. H. Villiers, Esq.

VIII. How far have the Civil Establishments of the several Residencies and Agencies been regulated, so as to secure efficiency and economy?

The political residencies and agencies established throughout Central India have undergone several modifications since 1818, in which neither efficiency nor economy has been lost sight of but it may be doubled whether either of these objects has been attained to the extent which is desirable.

Whatever destroys the unity of end in our political relations with these singular societies, cannot but be prejudicial; they are links in one great chain, though with a variety of often conflicting interests. In order, therefore, to maintain that uniformity which the treaties show to be requisite, unity of action must be secured, by placing the whole of our relations with the Rajpoot States under the control of one person thoroughly acquainted with their character and policy. While it appears advisable that the permanent camps should be strengthened, it is imperative to neutralize the feelings arising from the restraint they impose, so galling to a high-minded people, by a system of conciliation, and by continual efforts for their prosperity.

Ajmér, which is associated in the minds of these princes with all their earliest recollections as the seat of vice-regal government, appears the best adapted for the abode of a *"resident of Rajpootana."* There should be no resident agents at the courts of the native princes, each of whom should have a political deputation at Ajmér, consisting of one confidential chief, and a civil minister; the first to be appointed with the full consent of the council of chiefs belonging to each State.

The office of the "resident" being one of supervision and general control, a sufficient number of assistants should be placed under him, to conduct the duties of each State, and to present an abstract of all proceedings to the resident for his information and decision. *His* instructions should be conveyed to the vakeels through the assistants, while by the resident holding a *durbur* at fixed periods, at which all occurrences would be discussed in the presence of the vakeels and assistants, mutual checks would thus be imposed. As there can be nothing in the present state of our alliances to render secrecy necessary, this publicity would prevent any false reports being made by the vakeels to their masters; while it must increase the confidence of the native courts in our general political relations. To render this plan complete, all correspondence should be carried on in the vernacular dialects of the principalities, by which means the princes would be able to judge for themselves, instead of being at the mercy of some ignorant or unprincipled moonshee expounder of a foreign language. Nothing can be more absurd than that we should continue the use of the Persian language in these regions, in which not a word of it is understood; in fact, this principle should be extended to all countries with which we have transactions.

VI.
POLITICAL
OF
FOREIGN.
___
Appendix, No. 13.

Letter from
Lieut.-col. *Tod*
to
T. H. Villiers, Esq.

735-VI.   w

VI.
POLITICAL
OF
FOREIGN.

Appendix, No. 13.

Letter from
Lieut.-col. *Tod*
to
T. H. *Villiers*, Esq.

The assistants should be classed according to their rank and importance, perhaps as follows:

1st. Assistant for Méwar.
2d. For Marwar and Kishengurh.
3d. For Jeipoor and Shekhavati.
4th. For Harouti or Boondi-Kotah.
5th. For Jessulmér and Bikanér.
6th. For Sirohi, Dongerpoor, Bhanswarra, to which Satara might or might not be added.

A seventh might be added for Macherri, Kerewli, and the Jåt states of Bhurtpoore and Dhalpoor; but as their relations have been so long with Delhi, and their interests have thus become separated from Rajpootana, except on the score of unity, it might be desirable that they should remain distinct. From amongst the assistants the resident might be permitted to select one for the office of secretary, whose salary might be 500 rupees per month additional: which post would be an object of honourable ambition; it being however understood, that the Governor-General should always possess the *veto* on such appointment, to prevent its becoming one of favour.

The individuals selected as assistants should be men of talent, acquainted with the languages (more especially the vernacular dialects, and above all, having proper feelings of consideration for the people amongst whom they are to abide. It is essential that they be of an age when the principles and habits are fixed, and not, as is too generally the case, very young men, who obtaining the appointments through interest and favour, would regard them only as steps to advancement. Against this greatest of evils in all governments, but in a tenfold degree in these remote regions, we have especially to guard

If, in the ordinary judicial or territorial duties, a functionary from incapacity, or want of integrity, betrays his trust, the evil is remediable, as the mischief can only be transient and local; but it is far different in these regions, where the first error may generate evils that would sap the foundation of our power. It therefore behoves the controlling authorities at home to provide checks for such evils. All political officers are subject to the ordeal of an oath to withstand corruption, and to discharge their duties with energy and honesty. But there is no clause against moral unfitness, nor any requiring ability, temper, or taste for the peculiar functions of the office, while the individual is naturally apt to measure his own qualifications by the amount of salary in prospect.

It is the province of the Governor-General to administer the oath on all such occasions; and I would suggest, as a check to the abuse of patronage, that the Governor-General should himself, in the first place, take an oath before his council on every such nomination, that he believed the individual in every point of view qualified for the office.

It would not be possible, according to the present constitution of the civil service in India, to obtain from

VI.
POLITICAL
OF
FOREIGN.

Appendix, No. 13.

Letter from
Lieut.-col. *Tod*
to
T. H. *Villiers*, Esq.

735-VI.   w 1

VI.
POLITICAL
OF
FOREIGN.

Appendix, No. 13.

Letter from
Lieut.-col. *Tod*
to
T. H. *Villiers*, Esq.

that branch men with the requisite experience, to whom these appointments would be worth holding, if economy is attended to, since to the highest of these political assistants I should propose 1,500 rupees per month, graduated down to 1,000. In whatever branch of the service, therefore, the necessary qualifications are to be found, from that should selections be made. But it is highly important that there should be few fluctuations; and that the individuals holding such appointments should consider them as the *ne plus ultra*; but the highest of these would not be accepted by a civilian of six years' standing; or, if accepted, he would be looking to something better just as he began to acquire a knowledge of his duties. For these reasons it will be evident that economy and efficiency will be best attained by the election of officers from the military branch of the service; upon which body the incentive to quality themselves for such situations would act most beneficially. The certainty of general eligibility on the score of talent and character alone, would prove a source of widely-extended emulation. To this day, although military men hold the majority of such appointments, they are considered as trenching upon the exclusive rights of the civilians, and hold them more on sufferance than sanction: but it is matter of record that such nominations arose out of imperious necessity, being in the very face of instructions from home, *i.e.* "that military men should not be eligible to such appointments." The cause of the exception must be sought in the constitution of the executive body of the Company; but were the invidious restriction publicly, as it has long since been virtually, renounced, it would act as a spur on the energies of hundreds of men, whose talents lie dormant for want of *hope* of ever being enabled to employ them honourably and advantageously.

We now come to an important subdivision of this question, namely, the political control over the Mahrattas, and other protected chiefs, east of the Chumbul.

It appears quite incongruous that a political authority, even of the second order, should be maintained at Holkar's court; and it is the less required from the continuity of the camp at Mhow. In like manner Bhopál might dispense with any distinct agency. The court of Sindia is the only one which cannot well be left without a resident agent; but, at the same time, it is not calculated for the residence of an officer having general control over all the interests between Rajpootana and Boondelcund, a combination of authority promising beneficial results. It might be imagined that this power might also be vested in the "resident for Rajpootana;" but the tendency of this course to revive the ancient intercourse between the Rajpoots and Mahrattas, is a powerful argument against it. The barrier of separation cannot be too strong or too wide. I should therefore suggest one superior political authority to superintend the varied interests laying between our Rajpoot allies and Boondelcund, *i.e.* to include Sindia, Holkar, Bhopál, and the petty Rajpoot subordinates of Kheechiwarra,

VI.
POLITICAL
OF
FOREIGN.

Appendix, No. 13.

Letter from
Lieut.-col. *Tod*
to
T. II. Villiers, Esq.

VI.
POLITICAL
OF
FOREIGN.

Appendix, No. 13.

Letter from
Lieut.-col. *Tod*
to
T. H. Villiers, Esq.

Omutwarra, Déwas, and the dislocated estates of Meer Khan and Ghuffoor Khan. A resident and three assistants might suffice for these duties, and one of these assistants might reside at the camp at Mhow, which would be sufficiently near to embrace all the duties required at Holkar's petty court. As it would no doubt occasion considerable irritation to Bhopál to have her political relations at all connected with Sindia's court, it might be advisable to transfer these entirely to the Boondelcund division. Bhopál has long been morally, and since 1818 politically, severed from the Mahrattas, and whatever would tend to their reunion must be deprecated. These suggestions are offered as a mere outline of a measure that may be considered worth attention.

IX. How far have the Residents and Agents been subjected to the necessary checks?

The checks upon the political acts of residents and agents have been, and are, necessarily slight. There is, in fact, no proximate check; and as instructions are founded upon the representations of the agents themselves, it is scarcely going too far to say that there never have been any adequate checks at all. If the system I have ventured to suggest in answer to the last Quere were adopted, a sufficient systematic check would be provided.

On pecuniary disbursements there are the usual checks of audit, as well as the imposition of an oath against corruption, which is administered to residents and to their assistants.

X. How far has the existing system of Indian Government, or Home Direction and Control, been successful, or calculated to succeed in maintaining the requisite vigour, constancy, promptitude and unity of purpose in the several gradations of government, direction, control or influence, and (if any) what change is necessary or advisable in the constitution of the Home or of the Indian Government?

VI.
POLITICAL
OF
FOREIGN.

Appendix, No. 13.

Letter from
Lieut.-col. *Tod*
to
T. H. Villiers, Esq.

That the existing system of Indian government is "calculated" to work well, so as to secure "the requisite vigour, promptitude, and unity of purpose in the several gradations of government," we have demonstration in three of the most tremendous conflicts that have assailed it. The wars of 1803 and 1817 against the Mahrattas, and the Burmese war of 1825, afford the most unequivocal proofs that the system possesses the essential properties of good government. If by "constancy" be implied the probable perpetuity of these properties, it is obvious that this must entirely depend upon the excellence of the subordinate parts, which again rest with those who have to provide for them. With directing minds, such as existed in the eventful epochs just adverted to, of whom it might be said they *created* whatever was wanting to their purpose, similar results on similar emergencies might reasonably be expected. Even with less commanding talents than were exerted by the governments during the last untoward conflict, material danger might not be apprehended.

735-VI.   w 3

VI.
POLITICAL
OF
FOREIGN.

Appendix, No. 13.

Letter from
Lieut.-col. *Tod*
to
T. H. Villiers, Esq.

The first object of attention is necessarily the *primum mobile*, which involves the consideration of "Home direction and control."

It must not be imagined because our old Mahratta foes, the Péshwa, Bhoonsla, Sindia, and Holkar, are either destroyed or humbled; the Nizam paralyzed by our subsidiaries; the Rajpoot States bound to us by ties of gratitude; and all the minor predatory hordes dispersed, that ordinary talents may now govern India. This opinion once acted upon must be fatal, for the quenching of the opposition to our power was nothing compared to the difficulty of maintaining it afterwards.

The checks upon the Executive Government are necessarily lodged exclusively with the "Home direction and control," and upon their choice of individuals for the performance of these high functions will the prosperity and stability of our Indian empire depend.

I would urgently suggest the expediency of abolishing all retiring pensions or largesses to our governments at the expiration of their service, however brilliant or useful. The system is fraught with incalculable evil; in illustration of which instances might be cited, where, from the individual being unconsciously biassed by such remote expectations, the efficiency of our army was crippled. With a commercial government like that of the East India Company, whose ruling principle must, and ought to be economy, there should neither be a premium in prospect for the fulfilment of duty, nor a penalty on its omission, where considerations of local expediency may induce a governor to postpone commands that might be noxious if fulfilled. The salaries are ample; and beyond them the only stimulant should be the honour which the office confers, and the distinctions from the sovereign, which always follow any extraordinary manifestation of zeal and talent.

Should this immense empire ever fall into the hands of a weak or irresponsible governor, it may be lost for ever. The first evil, indeed, may be in a measure compensated by an able and independent council; but irresponsibility might neutralize this check. Much however depends on the selection of the men who are associated with the supreme power. It may therefore be a subject worthy of consideration whether the council might not include a military man of rank and acknowledged talent, by which means the interests of the army, that main stay of our power, would be better attended to than if the "Home direction" were composed of military men. It would also be placing in the hands of the Court another facility for recompensing extraordinary merit, besides being a distinguished mark of favour to the army at large.

Of the Court of Directors itself it might be embarrassing to speak with the freedom that truth and the public good demand, but that general opinion inclines to great modifications in this body. The main qualification, that of a personal knowledge of India, has been too much neglected; for although a fusion of men of influence, versed in the higher branches of commercial economy,

VI.
POLITICAL
OF
FOREIGN.

Appendix, No. 13.

Letter from
Lieut.-col. *Tod*
to
T. H. *Villiers*, Esq.

735-VI.   w 4

VI.
POLITICAL
OF
FOREIGN.

Appendix, No. 13.

Letter from
Lieut.-col. *Tod*
to
T. H. *Villiers*, Esq.

and who have not visited India, may be desirable, it assuredly is not so, that such a class should hold, and for years maintain, the entire executive power, to the exclusion of those possessing the higher qualifications for government. The result of allowing the majority of the Court to consist of commercial men, must be the government of India on narrow commercial principles, instead of that enlarged policy which embraces all the objects of a magnificent empire.

Moreover, in the selection of commercial men, it is essential that they should not possess commercial interests at variance with those which they are bound to protect. It would be monstrous that a man with strong West India interests should impose restraints by his voice and influence, as a director and senator, on East India produce. Neither should any particular class or influence predominate amongst the Directors; yet the Committee to whom, as is well known, belongs the right of initiating, discussing, and I may add, of carrying, every point that involves the government of India, is often composed of individuals who know nothing personally of the country, or the different branches of the service.

It is only requisite to classify the materials of the Court of Directors into Mercantile, Naval, Civil, Military, and Miscellaneous, to perceive the purposes to which their varied experience must be applied, when the faulty construction of the Court at once becomes apparent. We should see the two first classes, *i.e.* the Mercantile and Naval, almost entirely composing the chief committee of correspondence, regulating the fate of 200,000 men; while the military men in the direction are attending to the shipping, or disposing of commercial investments! It would be more consistent that men who have passed their lives in political, judicial, revenue and military duties, should be called upon for the aid of their experience when fundamental details of government are discussed; and *vice versá* that the others should be appointed to mechanical functions of trade and shipping, with which they are well acquainted.

Of the Court of Proprietors, in fact the Company, we may say, that it is utterly useless for any purpose save that decreed by the Directors, to whom it is entirely subservient. It is notorious that no subject at all unpalatable may be initiated there with any prospect of being carried; for, to use a vulgar phrase, whatever the proposition, it can at all times be swamped by a snap of the finger. As long as patronage shall be distributed as at present, so long will this preponderating influence crush every other. There is no part of the whole system more requiring modification than that of the patronage. As a matter of course, the Directors provide their own families and relations with the best appointments. The civil service is accordingly filled and kept up chiefly by the kindred of a party, which must beget irresponsibility, indemnity for inefficiency, and undue influence in the service; for governors and councillors will always be swayed by the common impulses of humanity; and the only mode that seems calculated to

VI.
POLITICAL
OF
FOREIGN.

Appendix, No. 13.

Letter from
Lieut.-col. *Tod*
to
T. H. *Villiers*, Esq.

735-VI.   X

VI.
POLITICAL
OF
FOREIGN.

Appendix, No. 13.

Letter from
Lieut.-col. *Tod*
to
T. H. Villiers, Esq.

restore the equilibrium of independence is the abrogation of retiring pensions, as before suggested.

There is another point that calls loudly for remedy, resulting from this system of patronage. Officers may have served the Honourable East India Company for half a century, and yet know not how to procure a cadetship for their sons! Whether, in future, the patronage is to reside with the Directors, whether it be sold, or however otherwise disposed of, there should be a certain number of appointments reserved for the children or near relatives of those who have served the Company long and faithfully. Neither would this course be impolitic; for the native soldiery, who are creatures of sympathy and strong feeling, would rejoice to see the children of their old officers amongst them, thus keeping up ties of ancient standing.

I have, &c.

38, York-place,
Portman-square,
23 March 1832.

James Tod,
Lieut.-Colonel Bengal Army,
late Political Agent W. Rajpoot
States.

Index

About the Authors

Lloyd I. Rudolph (1927–2016) was Professor Emeritus of Political Science at the University of Chicago, USA.

Susanne Hoeber Rudolph (1930–2015) was William Benton Distinguished Professor Emerita at the University of Chicago, USA.

In 2014 the Rudolphs were awarded the Padma Bhushan, one of India's highest civilian honors, for literature and education, and the University of Chicago's Norman Maclean Faculty Award.

Susanne Hoeber Rudolph, Mohan Singh Kanota, and Lloyd I. Rudolph at Amar Singh's *chatri* (cenotaph) in 1971.